CW01308624

Guide Book
To The Indian War Battlefields
In
Eastern Wyoming, Nebraska,
And South Dakota

by

R. Kent Morgan

Bloomington, IN   Milton Keynes, UK
authorHOUSE®

AuthorHouse™
1663 Liberty Drive, Suite 200
Bloomington, IN 47403
www.authorhouse.com
Phone: 1-800-839-8640

AuthorHouse™ UK Ltd.
500 Avebury Boulevard
Central Milton Keynes, MK9 2BE
www.authorhouse.co.uk
Phone: 08001974150

This book is a work of non-fiction. Unless otherwise noted, the author and the publisher make no explicit guarantees as to the accuracy of the information contained in this book and in some cases, names of people and places have been altered to protect their privacy.

© 2007 R. Kent Morgan. All rights reserved.

No part of this book may be reproduced, stored in a retrieval system, or transmitted by any means without the written permission of the author.

First published by AuthorHouse 1/17/2007

ISBN: 978-1-4259-6842-7 (sc)

Library of Congress Control Number: 2006909679

Printed in the United States of America
Bloomington, Indiana

This book is printed on acid-free paper.

This book is dedicated with affection to my wife, Linda,
sons John, Richard, and daughter Christie,
daughter-in-law Cindy, son-in-law Dionne,
grandson Jesse and granddaughter Kate

In Memorial to all the
Soldiers, Native Americans, and Civilians
who participated in these conflicts

Table of Contents

Preface	ix
Chapter 1 Connor's Battlefield (NE Wyoming)	1
Chapter 2 City of Sheridan, WY	5
Chapter 3 Bozeman Trail (Eastern side of Big Horn Mts.)	8
Chapter 4 Fort Phil Kearny (North of Buffalo, WY)	12
Chapter 5 Fetternan's Massacre (North of Buffalo, WY)	16
Chapter 6 Wagon Box Fight (North of Buffalo, WY)	20
Chapter 7 Town of Buffalo, WY (Gatchel Museum)	24
Chapter 8 Crazy Woman Fight	26
Chapter 9 Hoof Prints of the Past Museum (Town of Kaycee, WY)	30
Chapter 10 Dull Knife Battlefield (West of Kaycee)	32
Chapter 11 Fort Reno & Fort Connor (NE of Kaycee)	38
Chapter 12 Fort Casper (Casper, WY)	44
Chapter 13 Fort Fetterman (Douglas, WY)	50
Chapter 14 Guernsey Trail Ruts & Register Rook (Guernsey, WY)	54
Chapter 15 Fort Laramie (Ft. Laramie, WY)	57
Chapter 16 Grattan Fight (Ft. Laramie, WY)	62
Chapter 17 Fort Robinson (Ft. Robinson, NE)	66
Chapter 18 Yellow Hand Fight (NW of Crawford, NE)	71
Chapter 19 Wounded Knee (East of Pine Ridge, SD)	77
Chapter 20 Slim Buttes (North West, SD)	83
Appendix # 1 Brief on Medal of Honor	86
Appendix # 2 Brief on the Indian Wars Campaign Medal	89
Appendix # 3 Biographies of Soldiers and Chiefs	91
Appendix # 4 Fort Laramie Treaty of 1868	117
Appendix # 5 Bibliographies	129
About Author	131

Preface

This Guide Book was written for those who are interested in touring the battlefields and forts sites of the American Indian Wars in eastern Wyoming, northwestern Nebraska, and northwestern South Dakota. The reason these Indian Campaigns were fought was political: a growing need for expansion (Manifest Dynasty) after the Civil War, the discovery of gold and the vision of connecting the east and west coast together via the railroad. There are several books that discuss the political issues that lead to the Indian Wars. To enrich your experience and adventure, I have included the locations of specific sites.

One should carry some basic items that will be extremely helpful:
1) Current Wyoming, Nebraska, and South Dakota road map
2) Common compass
3) Binoculars

Optional items:
1) Handheld GPS (some rental cars have a GPS feature)
2) Camera
3) My Guide Book for Eastern Montana titled "Our Hallowed Ground"

This book gives you battlefield locations via GPS coordinates (for isolated battlefield sites), compass headings, maps and driving directions to the most advantageous viewing points, conditions of roads leading to them, as well as some points of interest along the way.
To get an idea of which battlefields are closest and their locations, I would suggest looking at your map to determine where you will begin

your battlefield "tour". Then you can plan your adventure accordingly, depending upon where in either Wyoming or Nebraska or South Dakota to begin.

How you map your journey is up to you, the reader, but I have it laid out in the following sequence by chapter:

If you follow this route on your state maps, it forms a large circle from and to Billing, Montana. From Billings, take I-90 south towards Sheridan, WY, continue on I-90 to Buffalo, WY, continue south on I-25 to Casper.

At Casper you can either go west on State 220 to see Independence Rock or you can continue east on I-25 to Douglas, WY.

Continuing south on I-25 about 40 miles to US 26 going to Guernsey and Fort Laramie.

After seeing Fort Laramie and Grattan Fight sites continue east on I-25 to town of Lingle and take US 85 to town of Lusk then take US 20 to Fort Robinson, NE.

Continue east on US 20 to town of Crawford and take State 2 and 71 north toward the state line with South Dakota (Do Not Cross State Line). Please see the chapter #17 for specific directions.

Backtrack to Crawford take US 20 east to Rushville.

From US 20 take State 87 to Pine Ridge at Pine Ridge take US 18 East to a county road on your left hand side directing you to Wounded Knee see Chapter #18 for specific directions.

Backtrack to Pine Ridge you can go North to see Slim Buttes several ways but one route is from Pine Ridge taking US 18 & 385 North to Hot Springs and continue North through the Black Hills, Mt. Rushmore and Chief Crazy Horse Memorial on to Rapid City and connect with US 85 to Buffalo, SD then right on State 20.

Note: Slim Buttes is the sort of out of the way battlefield site. It is located in NW South Dakota on State 20 east between Buffalo and Reva, SD. See Chapter #19 for specific directions.

After seeing the monument for Slim Buttes and the surrounding land you can drive back to Buffalo and turn right on US 85 to Bowman in ND and take US 12 to Miles City, MT and I-94 back to Billings. For battlefield and fort locations in Eastern Montana see my guide book "Our Hallowed Ground".

I would prefer to drive to Buffalo and drive north on US 85 to Belfield and take I-94 to Glendive, MT, (see my guide book "Our Hallowed Ground" Chapter #8 talks about the Glendive Cantonment at Glendive, MT). Once on I-94 this freeway will take you west to Billings, MT., it is about a 4.5 hour drive to Billings from Glendive.

Chapters are set up according to the name of the battlefield, fort or cantonment, with locations and driving directions (with or without GPS position). A brief history is included, current pictures of the sites, the campaign name, pertinent date(s), principal commanders involved, forces engaged, estimated casualties, and Medal of Honor recipients. Also included are additional points of interest with their GPS positions, and other bits of information and historical trivia I have gathered while actually visiting these sites and interviewing ranch owners.

In Appendix #1 - A brief explanation regarding the Medal of Honor. There were 428 Medals of Honor awarded during the Indian War campaigns. This is twenty two percent of the total medals awarded since the Civil War.

In Appendix # 2 - A brief on the creation of the Indian Campaign Medal, authorized by Congress some 42 years after the Indian Wars began same medal as on the cover.

In Appendix # 3 - Biography of Officers and Chiefs. It has always been interesting to learn what happened to these soldiers and Native Americans subsequent to the Indian Wars. Where did their careers take them? What rank did they achieve at retirement? Where are they buried?

In Appendix # 4 - The Fort Laramie Treaty of 1868, hundreds of history books and articles reference the Indian Treaty of 1868, also known by its official name The Fort Laramie Treaty of 1868. The full text is provided for your review and information.

The Indian War Campaigns are located in a reasonably small area of Eastern Wyoming, South Dakota and Nebraska, and easily driven to, plus toured on foot with some basic preplanning. All battlefield sites can be visited in five or six days. Most of the battlefield sites are almost exactly as they were back in 1876 and 1877 it is except for some natural soil erosion, currently being used as range land, with two exception the "Connor's Battlefield" is a state park and the "Grattan Fight", this site is being cultivated.

You can drive, self tour and walk most of the above described battlefield sites except for Dull Knife Battlefield you can see the Monument and the Village site in front of the monument but to see the rest of it you need to contact Graves Family for private tour and it is worth every cent.

The Grattan Fight (actual location) is in the middle of a field but there is a monument beside the road at the edge of the field and an irrigation ditch.

Slim Buttes Battlefield site is on private land. There is a monument on State 20 and interpretive signs. You can see of the area of the battle site from the monument with strong binoculars.

Note: I might mention that the grave sites for the men that perished at the Fetterman Massacre are now buried at Little Bighorn National Cemetery in Montana. The men from the Gratten fight are buried at McPherson National Cemetery in Nebraska.

There is one trooper that was buried at the Dull Knife Battlefield near hospital point, actual grave site is unknown, but you will see hospital point on your tour.

Driving from one area to another in Wyoming, South Dakota, Nebraska, and Montana is very enjoyable, there is a variety of beautiful scenery: rolling prairie, awesome rock formations and wonderful wildlife, especially deer and antelope that abounds on the prairie as well as domestic livestock.

NOTE: Please be EXTREMELY cautious of wildlife when driving at night. My recommendation is to drive after dawn to dusk, even on the major freeways. If you think this is a joke, just count the number of dead deer on the sides of the roads. Due to mild winters the last few years, the deer population has grown immensely. Please use caution.

Another area of concern while driving is the county gravel roads. Although quite dusty, these roads are normally quite good. Use caution when driving over rises, stay on the right side of the road for local traffic and do not drive too fast for the road.

I would like to recognize several generous people who have inspired, encouraged, mentored, shared information, guided, and allowed me access to these various battlefields and fort sites: The late Lester Jens, Former Director of Prairie County Historical Society, Terry, MT; Adele Jens, Terry, MT; the late Gary Larsen, Director of Prairie County Historical Society, Terry, MT; Carol Larsen, Terry, MT; Kathy Iverson, Monroe, WA; Mark and Carol Morgan, Leesburg, FL; Martha V. Morgan, Beardstown, IL; Freddy A. Morgan, Beardstown, IL; John Luther, Hysham, MT; Putt and Judy Thompson, Crow Agency, MT;

A Special Thanks to Kristin Medley, Dana Bowman, and Kathryn Iverson, my editors.

The special art was drawing by Richard M. Morgan.

Certainly, tremendous thanks go to those historical authors for their many fine books about these Indian War Campaigns. Their individual efforts are very much appreciated by us that are students of the American Indian Wars.

I would encourage each of you to read enough to be familiar with what happened at each site, for this will add to the richness of what you actually see. I have included a brief, referenced the documents and footnoted. Enjoy your tour!

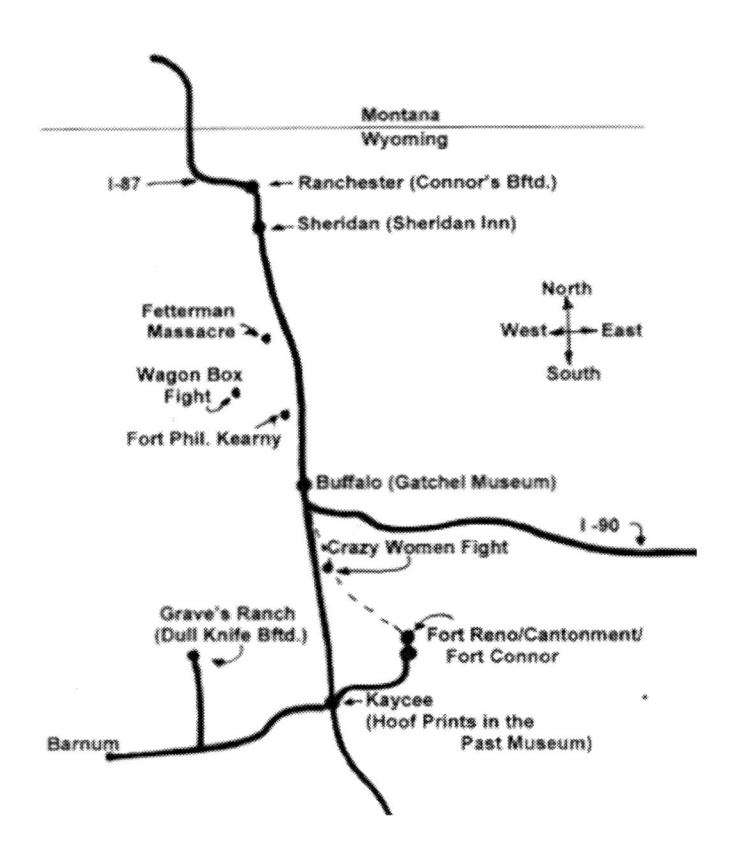

Chapter 1
Connor's Battlefield

Connor's Battlefield in Ranchester, Wyoming [1]

Other Names: Battle of Tongue River or Connor's Battlefield Site
Location: Ranchester, Wyoming, driving south on I-90 from Billings, MT Ranchester is the second exist off the I-90 driving south in Wyoming. It is 13 miles northwest of Sheridan, WY.
GPS coordinates off Highway: 44º 55.014N X 107º 09.122W Elev. 3894.

R. Kent Morgan

Drive down the hill into Ranchester. There are signs directing you to the battlefield state park. There is also a nice large sign explaining the battle on a main street corner before entering the park.

Campaign: Powder River Indian Expedition
Date: August 29, 1865
Commanders: Brigadier General Patrick E. Connor
    Chief Black Bear and Chief Old David of the Arapahoe

Forces Engaged: 558 Officers and Men with 179 Indian Scouts and 195 Teamsters [2]
    Approximately 400-500 Arapahos
Causalities: 5 troops killed and 7 wounded
    64 Arapaho's include son of Chief Black Bear killed
    7 women and 11 children taken captive but were released

In the summer of 1865, Brig. Gen. Patrick E. Connor was ordered by Maj. Gen. Grenville M. Dodge commander of Dept. of Missouri to conduct a punitive military campaign to suppress the hostile Sioux, Cheyenne, and Arapaho Indians who were harassing wagon trains along the Bozeman Trail.

Connor's command consisted of three columns: He led his column from Fort Laramie Northwest into the Powder River country. The Second Column commanded by Lt. Colonel Samuel Walker with 600 Officers and men led his command due north from Ft. Laramie. The Third Column commanded by Colonel Nelson Cole with 1,108 Officers and men proceeded from Omaha, NE NW on the east side of the Black Hills and then proceed west. Except for some minor skirmishes Connor's forces made little contact with the hostiles until late August.

Connor's Pawnee scouts discovered the village site on August 28, and with a night march Connor attacked the village around 7:00 am on August 29th. The Arapaho's were preparing to move camp when they were attacked. The soldiers overran the village site pushing the Indians 10 miles up Wolf Creek. According to Capt. H. E. Palmer, "Unfortunately for the women and children, our men had no time to direct their aim; bullets from both sides and murderous arrows filled the air; squaws and children, as well as warriors, fell among the dead and wounded." [2]

During this fight, other soldiers burned the camp and its supplies, making it a funeral pyre for their dead. Sixty four Indians were killed plus some 700 ponies. As the soldiers withdrew, the Indians advanced, recapturing several of their ponies, and continued harassing the column for several days. Connor column marched back to Fort Laramie following the establishment of Fort Connor (later Fort Reno Cantonment) on the Powder River near present day Kaycee.

It is said, that the Indians counterattack was so effective that the use of two artillery pieces saved the soldiers from disaster. Battle lasted until after dark but Connor's had destroyed the Arapaho's capacity to wage war and had killed over sixty Indians, including the son of Chief Black Bear. Following this skirmish, the Indians called Connor the "Red Devil" for his red hair. This engagement was a military victory and ended the Powder River Indian Expedition.

Connor's attack upon the Arapaho, caused them to join forces with the Sioux and Cheyenne at the Fetterman Fight in December, 1866. The Arapaho's were allies of the Sioux and Cheyenne and were present at the Battle of the Little Big Horn.

One Medal of Honor was awarded to Sgt. Charles L. Thomas who volunteered to locate and deliver a message from General Connor to Colonel Nelson Cole's column. His citation read, "Awarded for Heroism". [3]

The actual location of this small beautiful state park is in downtown Ranchester surrounded on three sides by the Tongue River. You can stay in your car as you drive around the park or walk it's very flat area, and a nice place for a picnic. You may want to visit the stone monument at the east end of the park indicating the approximate site of the village.

R. Kent Morgan

Historical Trivia:

While near Ranchester there are two more areas you might want to see. They are just east of Ranchester on Highway 14:

1. The Sawyer Fight – On August 31, 1865, an expedition was commissioned by the government to survey and build a road on the Bozeman Trail. The Arapahos attacked the group, led by ex-Lt. Col. James Sawyer in retaliation for the attack on Black Bear's village. After killing three of his men, the remaining 97 were pinned down for two weeks before being rescued by General Patrick Connor. The site is located four miles west of Connor Battlefield on Highway 14 where the present highway crosses the Bozeman Trail. There is a marker indicating the site.[2]

2. The Sibley Scout - July, 1867, Second Lt. Fredrick W. Sibley was order by Gen. Crook to conduct a scouting party while awaiting reinforcements at the Goose Creek Camp near to Sheridan, WY. Second Lt. Sibley led a party of 31 men. The Sioux spotted them and attacked, driving them into the Big Horn Mountains. Their only escape route started just outside Dayton most likely where the Bozeman crosses U.S. Hwy. 14 and wound up near Burgess Junction. [2] Here Sibley and his party were fired upon by the Sioux and at this point they abandoned their horses and retreated. They hiked over high, rugged mountains with just rifles and ammunition. The troops all suffered during this trying ordeal, but eventually did all survive to make it back to camp.

1.www.wyoshpo.state.wy.us/connor.htm
2.McDermott, Circle of Fire, Indian War of 1865, Pg. 77, 83 & 100
3.www.homeofheros.com/photo/1_indian/thomas_charles_afull,hmtl

Chapter 2
City of Sheridan

Other Names: None
Location: Sheridan, WY just off I-90 Freeway
Campaign: Yellowstone Expedition Camp
Date: June – August, 1876
Principle Commanders: Brigadier General George Crook, Commander of the Department of the Platte (present-day Iowa, Nebraska and Wyoming)

Forces Engaged: 1,300 men and Crow and Shoshone Scouts
Estimated Casualties: None

Sheridan was founded on May 10, 1882 by a pioneer John D. Loucks who named the town after his Civil War Commanding Officer Philip Henry Sheridan.

Sheridan Inn[1]

Sheridan Inn at 856 Broadway Street, constructed in 1893, was a premier hotel between Chicago and San Francisco. Famous guests included Presidents Theodore Roosevelt, Taft and Hoover as well as Will Rogers and Ernest Hemingway stayed there. The Inn was modeled after a Scottish hunting lodge with dormer windows on all 62 rooms. The Inn was partially owned by Buffalo Bill Cody in 1893 and he hired many people for his Wild West Show from here. It is a registered National Historic Landmark.[1]

The Inn also serves an excellent Buffalo Steak dinner if you're interested. They have many interesting pictures of the old west inside and the Inn can be toured. There is an old railroad Steam Engine directly across the street and a remodeled train depot.

It has been indicated that at this location is where General Crook set up his headquarters after his retreat from the Rosebud Battle. [2]

Crook's Battle of the Rosebud, June 17, 1876, with the Sioux, Cheyenne and Arapaho came eight days before the Battle of the Little Big Horn on June 25, 1876. The Battle of the Rosebud, was a tremendous all day battle involving some 2000 to 2500 men and warriors, with 9 troops killed and 17 wounded. Crook claimed victory because he maintained possession of the battlefield. The next day instead of marching north to make contact Gen. Alfred Terry marching along the Yellowstone River, Crook retreated south to the Sheridan area (called Camp Cloud Peak) to his supply train and remained in camp for eight weeks, nursing his wounded, reforming, waiting on reinforcements and ammunition.[3]

This essentially removed Crook's troops away from applying any pressure to the Indians from the south. Crook made no attempt to contact General Terry's Command during this time period.

On July 14, 1876 a courier from Terry's column made contact with Crook's command requesting he march north to make contact with Terry and Gibbon's columns on the Yellowstone River. The three couriers Private's James Bell, William Evans, and Benjamin F. Stewart carried dispatches to Gen. Crook were eventually awarded the Medal of Honor (see citations under appendix #3).[4]

---

1.   www.sheridaninn.com
2.   McDermott, Gen. George Crook's 1876 Campaigns, Frontier Heritage Alliance, Sheridan, WY, p.64
3.   O'neal, Fighting Men of the Indian War, p.99
4.   www.homeofheroes.com/photos/1_indian/evans_willams.html

Chapter 3

Bozeman Trail

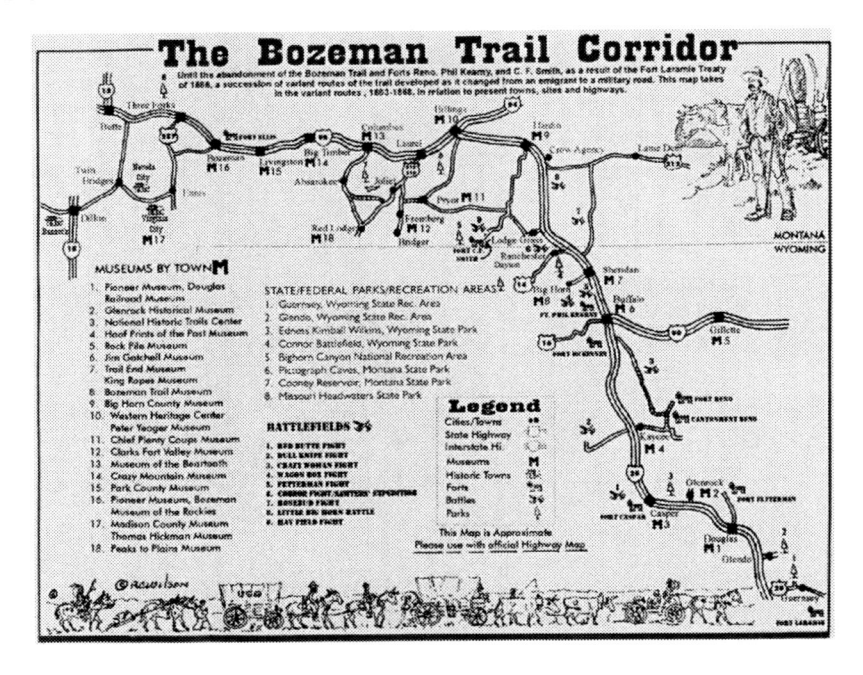

The Bozeman Corridor [1]

Other Names: Bloody Bozeman
Location: Extends from Deer Lodge, MT south to Fort Laramie, WY running south along I-90, I-25 and then along US-26
Campaign: Red Cloud War
Date: 1862 to 1866

Principle Commander: Gen. Connor, Col. Carrington, Gen. Wessells, and Gen. Crook
Chief Red Cloud

Forces Engaged: Several engagements along the trail
Casualties: Several Officers, soldiers and civilians

With the discovery of gold in present-day Deer Lodge and Bannack, Montana and ignoring current Indian treaties of the 1850s. John M. Bozeman and John Jacobs blazed the Bozeman Trail in 1862 from the Platte Road west of Ft. Laramie to the gold fields. This tail ran north along the eastern side of the Big Horn Mountains cut across the Powder, Big Horn and Yellowstone Rivers, then west to though the Bozeman Pass and to Virginia City, then north to Deer Lodge, cutting off 400 miles from taking the old Oregon Trail to the new gold fields.

The trail cut through the Lakota hunting grounds. In 1863-64 Bozeman led settlers and miners across the trail despite attacks from the Indians trying to protect their hunting ground. In 1864 as many as 1,500 people used this trail departed the North Platte River at Richard's Bridge east of present Casper and traveled the trail to the Montana settlements. The only encounter with local tribes was an attack by a large Cheyenne and Sioux war party against the Townsend train, on the Powder River east of present Kaycee, Wyoming.

Note: In 1867 John Bozeman was either killed by the Blackfoot Indians as reported by his then partner or possibly murdered by his partner.
In the terms of the Fort Laramie Treaty of 1851, the U.S. government had set aside the Powder River country, through which the Bozeman Trail ran, as Oglala and Brulé Sioux, Arapaho, and Cheyenne hunting ground. The various tribes objected to the trespassing and attempted to turn back their wagons. In 1865, responding to the demands of the settlers for protection, the U.S. Army sent 3 columns under General Patrick E. Connor to the region. Connor constructed a stockade, Fort Connors (later Fort Reno), 169 miles north of Fort Laramie at the forks of the Powder River, but his attempt to subdue the tribes failed.

Connor's fought the Indians at present-day Ranchester, WY (Chapter #1).

In 1866, the government ordered Colonel Henry B. Carrington (Chapter #4) to build three forts to protect the settlers traveling on the Bozeman Trail. He led the 2d Battalion, 18th Infantry, from Fort Laramie up the Bozeman Trail. Leaving one company at Fort Connor (now christened Fort Reno), Carrington proceeded sixty-seven miles to the forks of Piney Creek, near present-day Banner, Wyoming, where he established Fort Phil Kearny. In July, Carrington detached two companies under Captain Nathaniel C. Kenney to move even farther up the Bozeman Trail to build a third fort, C. F. Smith, ninety-one miles north of Phil Kearny, near present-day St. Xavier, MT. In June 1866, while a number of the Powder River chiefs were at Fort Laramie negotiating yet another treaty, Colonel Carrington was building two additional forts along the Trail.[2] The Indians would fight over this trail and the forts for the next two years. This was known as the Red Cloud War.

Both Forts were attacked repeatedly and there were standing orders that no person was go outside either fort without military escorts. Civilian Woodcutter and Hay cutter were consistently in peril of being cut off and attacked.

In December, 1866, led by Red Cloud fought a battle with a brash young Captain William J. Fetterman and 80 soldiers who were ambushed and all killed, known as Fetterman's Massacre, the Indians called this the Battle of the Hundred Slain.

Two years later the Treaty of 1868 (Appendix #4) was signed at Fort Laramie by Red Cloud and the forts along the Bozeman Trail were burned down by the Indians as the troops were being recalled to Ft. Laramie. This ended the Red Cloud Wars.

Red Cloud elected to live peaceably, for the rest of his life on his Reservation first located at Fort Robinson, NE (called Red Cloud Reservation and then Pine Ridge, NE). Other chiefs elected to pursue their traditional hunting and nomadic life style and follow their main food source the Buffalo.

1. www.bozemantrail.org
2. www.-cgsc.army.mil

Chapter 4

Fort Phil Kearney

Fort Phil Kearny sign [1]

Other Names: None
Location: Twenty one miles south of Sheridan on I-25 or 10 miles north of Buffalo, WY
Campaign: Bozeman Trail or The Red Cloud War
Date: June 17, 1866
Principal Commander: Colonel Henry Beebee Carrington (known by the Indians as "Little White Chief") [2]

Chief Red Cloud Principal Chief

Forces Engaged: Approximately 700 troops
Casualties: None

Ft. Phil Kearny was named for a Civil War Union General and constructed by Colonel Henry B. Carrington and the 18th U.S. Infantry in July, 1866, along the Bozeman Trail. You can see the traces of the building and fort's stockade.

It was the largest of the three forts constructed along the Bozeman Trail.

Fort C.F. Smith located some 91 miles north and just south of Hardin, MT, and Fort Reno near Kaycee, WY. Every time I visit the fort there is a new reconstruction. Our compliments to the Fort Kearny and Bozeman Trail Association who play a very active role in keeping this bit of history for our future generations to enjoy.

Colonel Carrington was ordered to establish three forts along the Bozeman Tail. He commanded the 2d Battalion, 18th Infantry Regiment, out of Fort Laramie. In addition to the 700 troops of the 18th, more than 300 women, children, sutters, and civilian contractors accompanied Carrington. The column included 226 mule-drawn wagons, the 35-piece regimental band, 1,000 head of cattle to provide fresh meat for the force, and all the tools and equipment necessary to create a community in the wilderness.

Carrington left Fort Laramie fully confident that he would be able to accomplish his mission without difficulty. Peace negotiations were taking place at Fort Laramie, and considering the number of chiefs participating, the prospect for an early settlement seemed good. Carrington was also well suited for his mission. A graduate of Yale, he was a practicing attorney when the Civil War began in April 1861. He volunteered immediately for service and secured a commission as a Colonel of the 18th Infantry upon its organization in May 1861. He was brevetted Brigadier General in November 1862. Although he saw no action with the 18th, he performed numerous staff duties efficiently and retained command of the 18th at the end of the war.

On June 28, 1866, Carrington's column arrived at Fort Connors (renamed Fort Reno), built the previous year by General Connor. Here,

Carrington spent ten days repairing, provisioning, and garrisoning the fort with a company of infantry. On 9 July, the remainder of the 2d Battalion left Fort Reno with all its equipment. Four days later, Carrington selected a site for the construction of his headquarters post and named it Fort Phil Kearny.

Carrington's chosen site lay just south of the point where the Bozeman Trail crossed Big Piney Creek. The narrow valley in which the fort sat was surrounded on three sides by high terrain. To both the north and south, the Bozeman Trail passed over ridges out of sight of the fort. To the west, the valley stretched five or six miles along Little Piney Creek before giving way to the foothills of the Bighorn Mountains. It was up this valley that the woodcutters and log teams would have to travel to provide the all-important building materials and fuel for the post's cooking and heating fires. Carrington's selection of this position has long been questioned. One weakness of the site was that the Sioux and Cheyenne continuously dominated the high ground and observed all movement into and around the fort. He was lucky that the Indians never had or could use cannons.

Construction of Fort Phil Kearny began as soon as Carrington's column arrived and continued almost until it was abandoned in 1868. The main post was an 800' X 600' stockade made by butting together 11-foot-high side-hewn pine logs in a trench 3 feet deep. The stockade enclosed barracks and living quarters for the troops, officers, and most of their families, mess and hospital facilities, the magazine, and a variety of other structures.

This is a huge stockade fort and is worth a walk around. I can still recall my first visit to the Fort in the 1996, when there was a gravel walkways and the flag pole in the center. It was late in the afternoon when I arrived and I walked southeast when I spooked three beautiful deer that gracefully leaped out of site across the creek. I thought not much had probably changed from when Carrington had arrived to the area.
During the brief two year existence, Ft. Kearny was a focal point of violent and constant battles with the hostiles. Upon the signing of the Fort Laramie Treaty of 1868, the 3 forts were abandoned and burned to the

ground by the Indians. The Bozeman Trail was situated in the middle of the migration path of the Indian main food source, the buffalo.

The years from 1866 to 1868 was known as "The Red Cloud War". Travel along the Bozeman Trail was an extremely dangerous experience. Chief Red Cloud refused to make peace until the trail and forts were abandoned. In May, 1868 the government ordered the fort to be abandoned and the Bozeman trail closed. In November, 1868 Red Cloud signed a peace treaty at Fort Laramie and he is the only Western Indian Chief to have won a war with the United States.

The Interpretive Center at the Fort is an excellent resource and has a good video that tells the story of the Ft. Kearny, Wagon Box Fight and Fetterman Massacre and they can provide you with a map to the Wagon Box Fight site.

Historical Trivia:

Sergeant George Grant was awarded the Medal of Honor for carrying dispatches from Fort Phil Kearny to Fort C.F. Smith in February 1867. His citation reads "Bravery, energy, and perseverance involving much suffering and privation through attacks by hostile Indians, deep snow, etc., while voluntarily carrying dispatches".[3]

Note: I might mention that the grave sites for the men that perished in the Fetterman Massacre and others have been re-interred at Little Bighorn National Cemetery.

1. www.philkearny.vcn.com
2. O'Neal, Fighting Men of the Indian Wars, p. 72-73
3. www.findagrave.com

Chapter 5

Fetterman Massacre

The FETTERMAN FIGHT
"The Fetterman Fight" by J. K. Ralston. Courtesy of FPK/BTA. 1

This is an excellent depiction of the ridge that Captain Fetterman and his troops died on. The soldier standing on the left side of the picture would be where the stone obelisk is located (see cover of book).

Other names: The Indians called it "The Battle of Hundred Slain or Battle of Hundred Hands" and Fetterman Fight
Location: Driving south 36 miles from Sheridan on I-25 you will see signs for Fort Phil Kearny, immediately after existing you will see signs to the Fetterman Massacre Site. This road way will lead you to the parking lot with a stone obelisk about 50 feet high.

Campaign: The Red Cloud War
Date: December 21, 1866

Principal Commander: Captain William Judd Fetterman

Chief Red Cloud, Crazy Horse, Wild Hog

Forces Engaged: 3 Officers, 27 cavalry, 49 infantry and 2 civilians
1500 to 3000 Sioux, Cheyenne and Arapaho
Causalities: 3 Officers and 78 Men killed
Unknown causalities with the Indians

On December 21, 1866 a wood party was attacked by the Indians. Captain William Fetterman led some 80 men out to relieve the wood party, and foolishly against Commanding Officer Colonel Carrington's orders, followed the Indians (led by Crazy Horse) over the Lodge Trail Ridge and into the valley. The Indians were led by Chief Red Cloud had laid an ambush for them. All the troops were killed and their bodies were mutilated horribly. [1]

As you walk from the monument to the northeast along the ridge path you can easily see the ambush ravines that the Indian would have hidden in. There are several interruptive signs along the path. On you left side or west side is a blacktop road but, of course back then would have been a very deep ravine. At one time several years ago you could have driven to Fort Kearney around Sullivant hill to the Wagon Box Fight location and then continued on the road which took you to the Fetterman site but now it is blocked off (I would suspect political reasons). Now you have to drive through Story after seeing the Wagon Box Fight or simply backtrack to Ft. Kearny and back to the freeway.

Following the Fetterman disaster, reinforcements arrived in January, 1867 commanded by Brig. Gen. Henry W. Wessells, who relieved Col. Henry B. Carrington of command. Carrington was reassigned to Fort Casper and was later assigned to Fort McPherson, NE for a Court of Inquiry. This inquiry ruined his military career. [2] Carrington tied for the rest of his life to vindicate himself but was unsuccessful.

After your visit at the Fetterman Site, just retrace your route and drive to Ft. Kearny a couple of miles away from Fetterman Massacre site.

Historical Trivia:
Stop to see John "Portuguese" Phillips Monument on the way as you proceed to Ft. Kearny. Portuguese Phillips volunteered to ride from Ft. Kearny to North Platte Telegraph Station to carry the news of the annihilation of Capt. William J. Fetterman and his command and to request reinforcements at the Fort.

John "Portuguese" Phillips Monument as you drive to Ft. Kearny [1]

Phillips volunteered to make this ride and carry Col. Henry B. Carrington's dispatches, about 190 miles in subzero weather. Some say he rode alone but he was accompanied by one Daniel Dixon to Fort Reno and by others along the way, including Robert Bailey. The pay for the service was $300 apiece for Phillips and Dixon, which they received in January, 1867. They arrived at Ft. Reno in the early hours of

December 23 rd Phillips was given an additional message to deliver to Col. Innis Palmer at Fort Laramie, thus extending their obligation.

According to the telegrapher at Horseshoe Station, Phillips, Dixon, and Bailey arrived about 10 A.M. on December 25th, when the dispatches were wired to the headquarters of the Department of the Platte in Omaha and then on to Washington Phillips went on to deliver the message to Fort Laramie, arriving at 11 p.m., where a full-dress Christmas Ball was in progress. The appearance of the huge form of Phillips, garbed in a buffalo overcoat, pants, gauntlets, and cap, quieted the festivities. His message caused preparations for a rescue party, delayed in departing by deeps snows until January 6th. In addition to receiving his pay, Phillips was given the best horse in Company F of the 2nd Cavalry. This ride from Ft. Kearney to Ft. Laramie is 236 miles in dead of winter.[2]

Although Phillips did not ride alone, he was built from what heroes are made of. There is also another plaque commemorating his ride at the curve going into Fort Laramie. No one can deny that he was not a courageous man even while receiving payment. Later the cavalry at Fort Laramie gave him one of their best horses.

---

1. www.philkearny.vcn.com
2. O'Neal, Fighting Men of the Indian Wars, p.114-115
3. www.johnsmilitaryhistory.com/fetterman.html excellent site

Chapter 6

Wagon Box Fight

Photo courtesy of Jim Gatchell Memorial Museum 2

Other Names: None
Location: 5 Miles west of Fort Phil Kearny
Campaign: Red Cloud War
Date: August 2, 1867
Principal Commander: Captain James Powell

Chief Red Cloud

Forces Engaged: 31 Soldiers and Civilians
1400 Sioux and Cheyenne
Casualties: 1 Officer and 2 soldiers killed and 2 wounded in corral.
4 Civilians killed in side camps

Estimated 60 Indians killed and 120 wounded. Note: In later years Red Cloud admitted that he had lost the core of his fighting force at that battle

Before you leave Fort Kearney get the map at the visitor center to the Wagon Box Fight which is only about a 10 minute drive and is worth seeing. It is well marked on the gravel road. Just proceed past the visitor center and follow the gravel road around Sullivant Hills on you right side.

Note: Sullivant Hills was named after Col. Carrington wife, her maiden name.

Note: Ft. Kearney, Wagon Box Fight and Fetterman Massacre sites are within a five mile radius. The road from the Wagon Box Fight will take to you Story, WY or you can backtrack to Ft. Kearney to get back on the I-25 Freeway to continue either north or south.

Throughout the spring and summer of 1867, the Indians had continued to harass the garrisons at Forts Smith and Kearny and morale was pretty low. None of the attacks had been seriously pressed, and neither side had sustained significant casualties. As a result of the Fetterman disaster reinforcements arrived in early January and Brig. Gen. Wessells relieved Col. Henry B. Carrington who was transferred to Ft. Casper and then Ft. McPherson awaiting a Court of Inquiry.

On August 2, 1867 a company of the 27th Infantry was guarding a wood cutting party. The woodcutters had removed the cargo wagon boxes from their wagons and arranged them in a circular corral. A large force of Sioux and Cheyenne attacked the corral for over 3 hours being repulsed by volleys from the newly issued breech loading rifles. There was a relief column sent out from Ft. Kearny with a cannon that fired air bursts over the Indians thus driving them away.

Because action had been sporadic, the Indians were unaware that early in July a shipment of 700 new M-1866 Springfield-Allin .50-70-caliber breech-loading rifles had arrived at the fort. The Springfield-Allin was a modification of the older .58-caliber Springfield muzzle-loader, the standard shoulder arm of the Civil War. Although single shot, the new rifle used an all-metallic .50-caliber cartridge, which was highly reliable and could be fired accurately and most important, rapidly. This was certainly a technological advancement that withstood 3 attacks of some 1400 hostiles with just 31 men.

Colonel John Eugene Smith, who had replaced Brig. Gen. Wessells on July 5, 1867 (who replaced Col. Henry Carrington in January) arrived with the wagon-train that also transported the newly modified rifles.[1]

On July 31, 1867, Captain James Powell led C Company, 27th Infantry, six miles from the fort to a wagon box corral to begin his thirty-day assignment as guard and escort for the civilian woodcutters. The corral was made by removing the boxes from atop the running gears of wagons. The running gears would then be used to haul logs from the forest to the fort.

The boxes, approximately ten feet long, four and one-half feet wide, and two and one-half feet high, were then placed in a rectangular formation approximately 60'X 30' forming the corral. A couple of the wagon boxes, with canvas still attached, held the rations for both soldiers and civilians and sat outside the corral. [1]

The Indians, their martial ardor stirred by a recent religious ceremony, attacked the soldiers at the corral on the morning of 2 August 1867 Powell had already sent out the working parties, which scattered when the Indians attacked. The Indians then turned their attention to the small detachment left at the corral. Over the next three hours, this small group of thirty-one soldiers held off hundreds of Indian braves. Finally, a relief party fired a mountain howitzer that surprised and dispersed the Indians. Powell credited his successful defense to the rapid fire of the breech-loading rifles, the coolness of his men, and the effectiveness of his position. This successful action was a badly needed tonic for the morale of frontier soldiers, who still smarted from the Fetterman disaster. Powell's small command had inflicted heavy casualties on the Indians and only lost three of his men.[1]

In spite of this small victory at the wagon box corral, the days of the Bozeman Trail were numbered.

---

1. Keenan, The Wagon Box Fight, p. 2
2. www.philkeary.vcr.com

Chapter 7

Gatchell Museum

Jim Gatchell Memorial Museum [1]

Other Names: None
Location: City of Buffalo, WY is on I-25 just south of I-90 junction, well noted on the map, city address is: 100 Fort St. and phone (307) 684-9331

Campaign: None
Date: Gatchell Museum opened June 17, 1956
Principal Commander: Founder James Gatchell
Forces Engaged: None
Casualties: None

The Gatchell Museum is one the finest I have seen for Indian artifacts and Pioneer implements. I would recommend it highly while visiting Buffalo.

Other sites in town would be the Fort McKenney (named after Lt. McKenney who was killed at Dull Knife Battle, south of Buffalo) now the site of the Veteran's Hospital.

---

1. www.jimgatchell.com

Chapter 8

Crazy Woman Fight

Crazy Woman Fight [1]

Other Names: Battle of Crazy Woman Fork of the Power River
Location: From Buffalo drive south on US 25 about 5 miles then take an exist (I think the Trabing Road, heading southeast which runs almost parallel to US 25. About 8 miles down this road you will pass along side the Crazy Woman Creek Fight.

There is a memorial monument on the creek bank about one-quarter mile downstream from the present bridge. Standing at the monument, one should look to the south, where a high point of a hill is the skyline. This is the place where Captain Templeton corralled the wagons for the fight. This site is also on BLM land. [4]

South of the creek on the land to the east of the road and just northwest of creek is a marker commemorating the Bozeman trail. The monument is on private land but it is accessible. There might be a charge for gaining accesses.[3] The Trabing Road is the old Bozeman Trail. Drive slowly to catch the Historical Sign.[2]

Campaign: Red Cloud War
Date: July 20, 1866
Principle Commanders: Lt. George M. Templeton, 18th Infantry
Forces Engaged: 2 Officers and 12 Troopers, 27 civilians including,
    9 women and children
    Unknown Indian forces
Estimated Casualties: 1 Officer and 2 Troopers killed
    Unknown Indians casualties

On July 20, 1866, Sioux and Cheyenne warriors attacked a small wagon train of soldiers and civilians under command of Lieutenant George M. Templeton who led 12 escort troops of the 18th Infantry with 27 civilians including 9 women and children. Templeton was courageous holding the train under siege until nightfall when a relief column came down the trail from Ft. Kearny to relieve the surrounded wagon train.

The battle began when Lt. Templeton and Lt. Napoleon H. Daniels rode ahead of the wagons to chase what appeared to be a herd of buffalo. As they entered the creek valley, the warriors attacked, killing Daniels with arrows and chasing Templeton back to the train. Templeton and the other officers corralled the wagons as the Indians pressed their attack. The situation was serious with a limited amount of firepower.

Wagons had been positioned in a low area, Templeton ordered them repositioned on a high bluff about a mile above the creek. This was done while still skirmishing with the warriors.

With the new position attained the battle had went on all day and ammunition was getting low. It was decided to send for help, and Reverend David White and a soldier slipped out and headed south to Fort Reno to get help.

A supply wagon train commanded by Captain T.B. Burrowes from Ft. Kearny was coming southbound and relieved the besieged Lt. Templeton's group. One soldier Lance Corporal Terrence Callary was killed from Burrowes command and was buried by the corralled wagons by this time the Indians had dispersed.

Lt. Daniel's body was recovered and transported to Fort Reno for burial. This was the beginning of hostilities along the Bozeman Trail that would last for the next two years ending with the Fort Laramie Treaty of 1868. Crazy Women Creek was an especially dangerous spot for travels along the trail.

Lt. Daniels & Sergt. Terrel's marker at Crazy Women Creek [3]

1. www.philkearny.vcn.com
2. www.americanindian.net(phil Konstantin, 2003 vacation)
3. www.lakotatour.itgo.com
4. Murray, Robert A., The Bozeman Trail, Highway of History

Chapter 9

Hoof Prints of the Past Museum

Hoofprints of the Past Museum Building [1]

Other Names: Kaycee Museum
Location: Kaycee, WY on I-25 some 45 Miles south of Buffalo, at 344 Nolan Ave.
Campaign: None
Date: None
Principle Commanders: None
Forces Engaged: None
Casualties: none

Kaycee offers an excellent Museum called the "Hoof Prints of the Past" and it is today a crossroads, to the "Dull Knife Battlefield" and "Whole in the Wall" to the west and "Fort Reno" and Fort Connor in the East.

The Museum can coordinate two tours for you if you wish:
1. "The Dull Knife Battlefield"
2. "The Whole in the Wall"

The "Hoof Prints of the Past Museum" phone numbers are (307) 738-2381 or (307) 738-2570. You must call ahead for booking these tours.

You can book a private tour of "The Dull Knife Battlefield" by calling Ken and Cheri Graves Ranch at (307) 738-2247 to coordinate time and date.

The battlefield is located on their ranch. I took a private tour with Cheri Graves and she provides an excellent, comprehensive battlefield historical tour of the entire site. The battlefield location is isolated but it is a wonderful drive, seeing the wild life, beautiful red rock canyons and buttes is worth every minute and opportunity to tour this famous battlefield where the Northern Cheyenne were defeated. I consider this a must see if you're a military historian. This area is very rich in Indian and outlaw history.

During my tour I started out very early on a September morning and must have seen at least 200 magnificent deer, an eagle, wild turkeys, and coyote just on the way out. At one point I had to stop for I was surrounded by these beautiful deer.

I would also recommend you purchase the book "Dull Knife Battlefield" by Mr. Fred H. Werner from Cheri Graves if she has any left, the one I bought was autographed by Mr. Werner and Cheri Graves, it is an excellent book who did outstanding research at the Dull Knife Battlefield.

---

1. www.hoofprintsofthepast.org

Chapter 10

Dull Knife Battlefield

Dull Knife Battlefield looking northeast [1.]

Other Names: None
Location: Traveling south on I-25 and take the Kaycee exist there is "7-Eleven" Convenience Store just across from the exist. Take a right turn after existing and continue west on county road #190 directly in front of the "7- Eleven" for approx. 1 to 2 miles.

Take the first black top road to your left. Notice the pole with several Ranch signs, look for Graves Ranch Sign. From this Ranch sign, it is 24 miles to the battlefield. Continue along this paved road for 16 miles, you will come to a huge Red Rock (this rock is at least one story high) at coordinates:

GPS 43o 39.411N X 106o 54.237W, Elev. 5099

Take a right at the huge rock (you will be heading North) and continue to the end of the road (this road is gravel and dirt) another 8 miles to Ken & Cheri Graves Ranch Gate, the coordinates:

GPS 43o 45.283N X 106o 57.253W, Elev. 5786

Note: There are several Graves (families) that live next to the gravel and dirt road but, continue to the end of the road. On your right side there are magnificent Red Rock canyons.

Campaign: Big Horn Expedition 1876
Date: November 25, 1876 (Thanksgiving Day)
Principal Commanders: Brigadier General George Crook, Commander of the Department of the Platte (including present-day Iowa, Nebraska, and Wyoming) and Colonel Ranald Slidell Mackenzie, Fourth Cavalry

Chief Dull Knife, Principal Chief
Chief Little Wolf, Principal War Chief

Forces engaged: Troops: 1,100 Officers and Men of which 360 were Indian Scouts including Pawnee, Ute, Shoshone, Crow and even a few Cheyenne Indians.

1,400 Cheyenne, approximately

Estimated Casualties: 1 Officer and 6 Soldiers were killed (one Pvt. Beard, was buried on the battlefield at Hospital Hill) and 26 wounded.

25 Indians confirmed killed, suspected many more died from exposure during their retreat.

Orientation to the Battlefield:

At the Graves Ranch Gate, you can look to your right or due east and will see the Dull Knife Battlefield Monument, it is perhaps 150 yards off the road and can easily be walked. The monument is getting tough to read now, but it says:

"Here Nov. 25. 1876 Gen. R. S. Mackenzie with U.S. Forces Composed of detachments of the 2nd, 3rd, 4th, 5th, Cavalry: 4th, and 9th Artillery: 9th, 23rd, Infantry defeated the CHEYENNES under Dull Knife, Lieut. McKinney and six soldiers' were killed in battle".

The cliff just in back of the monument, is the same cliff that the Shoshone Scouts led by Lt. Walter S. Schuyler were positioned to shoot down on the Cheyenne village, battlefield and Indians trying to escape. This is now known as Mackenzie's Mountain. Note: This can be toured also, I believe with Sheri Graves.

If you turn your back to the monument, looking northwest just 50 yards to the front, was the location of the Northern Cheyenne Village site. Beyond the village site across the creek perhaps 500 yards was the actual battlefield that was charged by Colonel Ranald Mackenzie's troops at day break on 11-25-1876 (Thanksgiving Day).

The mountains directly across the valley are called the Fraker Mountains and to your left in the distance are the Big Horn Mountains.

Also on your left you can see the high ridge above the battlefield or valley floor. It is this location where the breastworks were constructed by the Cheyenne who fired down on the troops. This was done so that their women, children and old people could escape over the Fraker and into Big Horn Mountains directly across the valley. Cheri Graves can take you to this ridge to see the breastworks and to see the escape route just behind the ridge.

The Battle:

On November 23, 1876, General George Crook ordered his second in command Colonel Ranald Mackenzie to take the scouts and all the cavalry except one company and to find the Cheyenne Indian camp in the upper valley of the Red Fork. They sought to destroy their village and bring the Indians back to the reservation.

Mackenzie's force marched at night through the narrow canyons and very difficult terrain of the Big Horn Mountains to attack the village. At dawn on November 25, 1876, the command readied itself for a charge on the village. A reconnaissance was taken and discovered that the Cheyenne were having war dances in four locations. The scouts reported there were at least three pony herds.

As dawn appeared, the dancing stopped and the Indians had retired to rest. Although the village had been warned previously by Cheyenne Scouts of Mackenzie's approach, the attack was a surprise. As Mackenzie's main force approached the village a large number of Indians took positions in a deep ravine and were firing to run off pony herd from the plateau above the village on which the soldiers were concentrating. Mackenzie ordered two officers to charge the ravine with their companies and cut off the advance of the Cheyenne there.

It is here that Lt. McKinney was mortally wounded and 6 other troopers with minor wounds. The troops were ordered to burn the village and supplies, and capture as much of the pony herd as possible. Later the horses were divided up among the Indian scouts.

The heaviest firing dropped off around 11:00 AM and continued sporadically throughout the day and into the night with the Indians escaping into the Big Horn Mountains.

Some 25 Cheyenne men, women and children were killed. Mackenzie sent out scouts in the morning of the 26th to ask the Cheyenne to surrender but they would not answer. The tribe escaped with only the clothes on their backs and what few provisions they gathered along with several horses. They killed the horses and ate them to survive. They trudged northward for two weeks through the snow and subfreezing temperatures to reach their only source of help, the village of Crazy Horse in the Wolf Mountains. Several people, mostly children, died along the way. Crazy Horse took in the surviving refugees, feeding, clothing and sheltering them as best he could. Crazy Horse's own people could not keep up such support for long; they themselves were suffering. Some of the Northern Cheyenne left the village to surrender to the whites at Camp Robinson in early spring.

Mackenzie's attack on Dull Knife's village destroyed all the Indians Teepee's (TP's) and supplies and with the lack of game that winter convinced many of the Lakota leaders on the Tongue River to pursue peace. Crazy Horse, who's following at the time consisted of about 250 lodges and after a battle with Col. Nelson A. Miles on Jan. 8, 1877 in the Wolf Mountains, just south of present day Birney, MT [2] he too surrendered at Ft. Robinson in May, 1877.

Mackenzie left the battlefield at noon on Sunday the November 26, 1876. He packed out his remaining dead and wounded by horse. The dead were buried at General Crook supply camp and Lt. McKinney body was taken to the railroad and shipped to his relatives in Memphis, Tennessee.

First Sergeant Thomas H. Forsyth, Co. "M", 4th Cavalry was awarded the Medal of Honor for gallantry in this action he was the only recipient.

Historical Trivia:

When across the creek near the base of the ridge, asked Sheri Grave to show you the TP rings. Also in the same area as the TP rings you will notice the flakes of flint indicating where the ancient Indians knapped stone arrow points. When the Indians camped and the ground was frozen they would roll large stones to keep the edges of the TP secure to the ground. When they left to move to another camp they simply rolled the stones aside to be used the next time they camped there, thus forming TP rings.

1. www.wyshpo.state.wy.us/dullknif.htm
2. Morgan, R. Kent, Our Hallowed Ground, Page 58
   Warner, Fred H., The Dull Knife Battle

Chapter 11

Fort Reno & Fort Connors

FORT RENO

First Fort on the Bozeman Trail [1]

Other Names: Fort Connor, and Reno Cantonment
Location: From Kaycee to Fort Reno is 17.7 miles of good blacktop road. At Kaycee drive east on county road 192 to the Lower Sussex Road and take a left, (driving north) for 5.1 miles you will come to 3 historical plaques describing the earlier Fort Reno Cantonment. This also could have been the location of Fort Connors that was established as a supply depot in the 1860's:

GPS coordinates 43o 46.927N X 106o 16.091W, Elev. 4363.

Continue to drive north another 3 to 4 miles and see 3 more historical plaques indicating location of Fort Reno during 1876 Crooks expeditions:
GPS coordinates 43o 49.739N x 106o 14.501W, Elev. 4322.

The monument stone below is at GPS coordinates 43o 49.685N X 106o 14.368W, Elev. 4320.

Campaign: Connors' Powder River Indian Expedition 1865, Crooks' Powder River Expedition March, Yellowstone Expedition, June, Big Horn Expedition, November, 1876.
Date: August 29, 1865 and year of 1876
Principle Commanders: Brig. Gen. Connors in 1865, Col. Carrington, 1866, Col. James Van Voast, 1867
Forces Engaged: Amount varied depending on expedition or along the trail
Casualties: None

During the summer of 1866, Colonel Henry B. Carrington of the 18th U. S. Infantry led a force of 700 men into the Powder River country to begin construction of the new posts. Carrington reached Fort Reno on June 28, 1866. Originally called Fort Connor, the post was located on a high plateau on the banks of the Powder River near the mouth of Dry Fork. Fort Connor was established on August 14, 1865 by General Patrick Connor during the Powder River Expedition of that summer.

November 11, 1865 the Fort's name changed from Connor to Reno in honor of General Jesse L. Reno, killed September 14, 1862 at the Battle of South Mountain in the Civil War. The post was a crude affair with a warehouse and stables surrounded by a rough cottonwood log stockade. The quarters of both the officers and men were without protection. The buildings had earth covered roofs and dirt floors. Company C and D, 5th U. S. Volunteers, and Company A, Omaha Scouts, garrisoned the fort during the winter of 1865-66 but upon Carrington's arrival they were mustered out of the service and departed "without a single regret".[1] It was one miserable place to be posted.

The two years that followed saw troops from Fort Reno engaging in the routine duties of garrison life interspersed with more exciting moments involving Indian warfare. The Fort never came under direct attack from the Indians but encounters with them occurred regularly throughout the area and along the trail to the north and south. The Indians frequently ran off stock, both civilian and military, harassed the emigrant trains, and killed a number of individuals who had wandered from the safety of their respective groups. Unlike Fort Phil Kearny, Fort Reno never gained widespread publicity, notoriety, or folklore fame. This was due in large part to the fact that troops from Fort Reno never participated in any major encounters. Fort Reno's role consisted primarily of insuring that the southern section of the Bozeman Trail was kept open and passable.

Throughout its existence Fort Reno experienced numerous additions, improvements and modifications in its physical layout. Connor's men first built a small stockade of cottonwood logs about 120 feet square. The eight to ten inch logs were set four feet deep in a trench leaving a wall about eight feet high. Inside the stockade was built a quartermaster's and commissary storehouse. Other buildings put up outside the stockade during the fall of 1865 included two barracks, two officers' quarters, a post hospital, shops, teamsters quarters, and two sutter's buildings. Under Carrington's command in 1866 a log stockade was placed around the unprotected garrison buildings complete with log bastions on the northwest and southeast corners. A sturdy adobe for commander's quarters was also built during 1866. In 1867 Commander James Van Voast relocated the entire west stockade line, tore down the old bastions, and built three new hexagonal blockhouses, a new square bastion, and relocated several of the gates. The construction of a guardhouse and additional warehouses rounded out the improvements. No further building was done at Fort Reno prior to abandonment in 1868. In accordance with the Fort Laramie Treaty of 1868, Fort Reno was abandoned in August, 1868. Shortly after the military left, the entire post was destroyed by fire compliments of the Indians. Bodies left in the post cemetery were later re-interred and placed at the Custer Battlefield National Cemetery during the 1880s.[1]

View of the Powder River from the fence line.

Just across the road you can walk around the actual fort grounds and down to the Powder River. There is a Memorial Stone at the location of the actual fort. When I walked the area there was lots of broken cast iron from the fort's stoves, glass and china chards lying around the ground, which you should not take. You can easily see down to the Powder River approximately 50 yards north of the Memorial Stone along with a roadway coming up to the Fort from the river.

This fort was build mostly out of adobe/sod and cotton wood logs and has long since melted down to lumps of sod but it is fun to walk over the site.

Here is an excerpt from a museum sign from which I can't remember where is titled: " Life at the Fort"

> "Life at the fort was characterized by isolation and tedium. The post was dependent upon either the river or the overland trails for communication and transportation, both of which were intermittent due to weather, fluctuating river levels and Indian intervention. As a result, mail delivery and supplies were limited or unavailable.
>
> Living conditions at the post were fair at best. The barracks and other buildings were hastily constructed using poor materials and unskilled labor. Daily life was tedious routine – beginning at 5:30AM and ending at 9:30 PM. Fatigue duty, such as haying, wood chopping, and water hauling, constituted most of each day and left little time for purely military tasks. Located far from "civilization," the soldiers and civilians at the post had to find or make their own entertainment, which varied according to the resources available. This often meant consuming a fair amount of ale and spending a good deal of time with Indian women and post laundresses. Extremes in weather and climate, poor hygiene and poor diet contributed to the ill health and low morale of many soldiers at the fort.
>
> Because the army only provided the very basic in food and clothing, the soldiers relied heavily upon the post trader for personal items. No other source of these items was available, however, and the soldiers were at the mercy of the trader's prices. Other entrepreneurs, including tailors, barbers, and restaurateurs, were allowed on post as long as they obeyed military regulations and did not compete with the post trader. It wasn't until the coming of the railroad in 1887 that access to the outside world became readily available and life at the fort was more comfortable and relaxed. " [1]

---

1. www.wyoshpo.state.wy.us/fortreno.htm

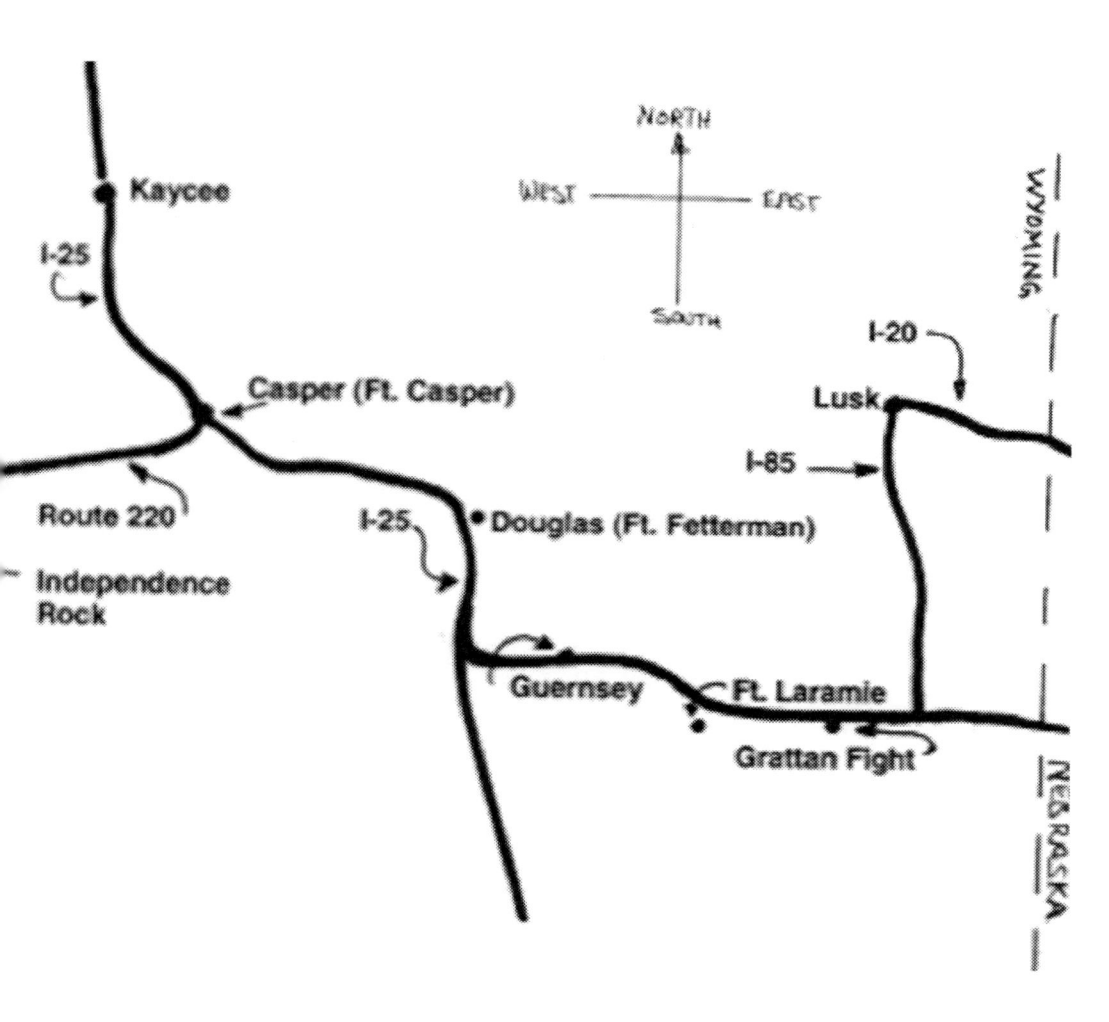

Guide Book To The Indian War Battlefields In Eastern WY, Neb. & SD

Chapter 12

Fort Casper

Fort Casper 1865 military post located on the North Platte River a major river crossing on the Oregon, California, Mormon Pioneer, Pony Express, and transcontinental telegraph trail corridor.[1]

Other names: Platte Bridge Station
Location: 4001 Fort Casper Road, Casper, Wyoming, as you enter Casper just follow the Fort Casper road signs and it will lead you right to the museum and to the fort. The Fort has an excellent book store.

Campaign: Red Cloud War

Date: 1863-1866
Principal Commanders: Lt. Col. William O. Collins
   Major Anderson after Lt. Col Collins left
Forces Engaged: 31 Troops engaged
   Estimated 100 Indians

Casualties: 1 Officer and 27 Troopers killed
   Unknown number of Indians

Lieutenant Colonel William O. Collins received orders on June 3, 1862 to proceed with three companies west along the trail to South Pass. His orders were to protect the employees and property of the Overland Mail Company and the Pacific Telegraph.

During the first week of June 1862, the troops from Company D, 6th Ohio Volunteer Cavalry (O.V.C). began establishing an outpost near Guinard's bridge. Soldiers spent much of the summer repairing the telegraph line damaged by Indians. The raiding was so successful that on July 11, 1862, the Postmaster General of the United States ordered all mail carriers to abandon this portion of the route in favor of the Overland Trail through southern Wyoming.

By the end of 1862, Platte Bridge Station had taken shape. In July 1863, Collins organized a Second Battalion of O.V.C consisting of Companies E, F, G, and H. Because his regiment was 50 men short when he recruited the new companies in 1863, Collins gave Confederate prisoners of war a chance to join. Men enlisted in this manner were known as "Galvanized Yankees." By October 10, the troops arrived at their new posts.

In response to the 1864 Sand Creek Massacre of Black Kettle's Cheyenne by Colonel Chivington's militia in Colorado Territory, Plains tribes increased raids along the trails the following spring. In July 1865, the hostiles gathered to attack Platte Bridge Station.

On July 26, 1865, Lieutenant Caspar Collins (son of Lt. Col. William O. Collins, former Post Commanding Officer) led a small detachment a mile north, from Platte Bridge Station to escort an army supply train traveling from Sweetwater Station. Less than a mile from the bridge, Collins' men were ambushed and had to fight their way back to the fort. Five soldiers including Collins were killed in the Battle of Platte Bridge.

Sergeant Amos Custard and 24 men with the supply wagons from Sweetwater Station were attacked later that same day five miles west of the fort. Only three soldiers survived the Battle of Red Buttes.
In the fall of 1865 the additional reinforcements arrived and a new fort was constructed. Over the next two years, the army built more than 20 new buildings to house 400-500 soldiers. By Special Order 49 dated November 21, 1865, Major General John Pope changed the name of Platte Bridge Station to Fort Casper, misspelling the fallen lieutenant's name. Pope chose the lieutenant's first name because there already was a Fort Collins in Colorado named for his father.

On June 28, 1866, Captain Richard Morris of the 18th U.S. Infantry took command of Fort Casper. With the railroad and new transcontinental Telegraph in southern Wyoming Ft. Casper was abandoned in Oct. 1867, with the troops and useful material including some building transferred to Fort Fetterman.

Homesteaders and ranchers arrived in the Casper area by the late 1870s, and the grounds of Fort Casper became part of the CY Ranch. In 1936, Casper citizens and the Works Progress Administration reconstructed Platte Bridge Station using sketches made by Casper Collins and others in the 1860s. Reconstructions of the Mormon ferry and a section of the Guinard bridge are also part of the site.[1]

Note: After taking in Fort Casper, you could take a side trip to Independence Rock and Devil's Gate. After leaving Fort Casper take highway 220 west approx. 2-4 miles, there is a stone monument on the right hand side of the highway, for the site of the Battle of the Red Butte across the river. This was where Sgt. Custard and 21 men of his wagon train were killed by Indians. The 22 men's graves have never been located.

Continue on Highway 220 to Independence Rock. It is 73 miles west of Casper it is here that the pioneer wanted to be on or before July 4th of that year, so as to make it across the mountains into Oregon or California before winter set in. It is here that they rested, repaired wagons, celebrated the 4th of July, and carved their names on what is known as Independence Rock.

You can't miss "The Rock" just beside the highway. Your welcome to walk around to east side (there is a gradual slope and you can easily ascend to the top. Perhaps a 100 yard gradual climb to the top at an easy angle to assent. On top you have an excellent view of the surrounding area and read the hundreds of names and dates carved by those courageous pioneers in this huge granite rock.

Note: There is a book published by the Wyoming Historical Society in Casper that has the names and locations of all pioneer names carved on the rock.

You can see Devils Gap from Independence Rock and it is just 3 miles away and well worth the look. This trail was taken by the pioneers. It was here in 1850 that several hundred Mormons were trapped in a winter blizzard and perished. They are buried along the trail and on the hillside that you're walking on.

Historical Trivia:

A personal note: I had heard from my family several years ago about a pioneer Uncle and family that traveled west in a wagon train in early 1800's and about a baby that had died on the way and was buried near Mount Hood in Oregon.

Many years ago I wanted to investigate this bit of family information. I drove down to Oregon City (End of the Oregon Trail) from Seattle and talked with a couple of historians at the Oregon City Museum. I didn't have much to go on but told them what I had heard. They referenced the "Barlow Trail" and "Government Meadows". They recommended the book "Historic Sites Along the Oregon Trail" book and sure enough

Baby Morgan's grave site was listed along with her mother Rachel. This was quite a find for me and started my journey.

I might make a note here that the history along the Oregon Trail is very interesting and the book noted above is truly excellent for anyone wanting to travel along the trail today.

In 1847 a fifth generation Uncle Daniel Morgan, his wife Rachel, and 2 sons from Cuba, Illinois traveled West on the Oregon Trail to claim free land in Oregon. Their wagon train was captained by Rachel father Woodsides, which paralleled the Mormon Wagon Train of 1847 with Brigham Young. This was the famous exodus from the Nauvoo, Illinois to the founding of Salt Lake City, Utah.

After arriving at Independence Rock in June, Daniel's wife Rachel Woodsides Morgan gave birth to a baby girl but, due to child birth complications Rachel died and is buried on the southeast side, between the Rock and the Sweetwater River. Her grave, unfortunately is not marked. One would think that at least someone would have carved her name in the rock but, I could not find any evidence of this after visiting the site twice. I also purchased a book from the Historical Society that lists all the pioneers' names on the rock but, unfortunately Rachel's was not referenced. Her burial was witnessed by two Mormon men (John Brown and Wilford Woodruff) who had climbed the rock. They both documented her burial by name in their journals. [2]

Also referenced in the book above is the referenced the location of Baby Morgan's grave site is at Government Meadows/Summit Meadows. [2] On October 24, 1847 she was accidentally killed when she was unloaded and placed under the wagon to shade her from the sun. The wagon load shifted causing the tailgate to fall, striking her in the head. She now rests besides a huge glacial boulder with a brass plaque presented by the family in Aug. 20, 1957, marking her grave in Government Meadows at the foot of Mount Hood in Oregon. There are three other burials within a 20 foot square fencing nearby.

The Plaque reads "This marks the grave of Baby Morgan Infant Daughter of Daniel and Rachel Woodsides Morgan born near Independence Rock, June 1847. The baby died as a result of an accident and was buried here at Summit Meadows Oct. 24, 1847. Burial witnessed by Jacob and Sarah Woodsides Caplinger 'Sweetly Rests Our Baby Dear All The Labors Ceases Here Far From Home Though Laid To Sleep Loving Hearts They Memory Keep'.[2]

1. www.cityofcasperwy.com/content/leisure/fort/Outreach.asp
2. Haines, Historical Sites Along the Oregon Trail, p.414-416

Chapter 13

Fort Fetterman

Reproduction of Fort Fetterman Officers Quarters on the plateau [1]

Other Names: None
Location: Located 7 miles north of Douglas, Wyoming on Highway 93, take Exit 140 off US 25. At the first stop light, turn left and you should be heading north on Highway 93 and just follow the Fort Fetterman signs to the park, it is on the right side up on a plateau.

Campaign: Powder River Expedition (March, 1876), Yellowstone Expedition (June, 1876), Big Horn Expedition (November, 1876).
Date: 3 Expeditions in 1876 were staged from Ft. Fetterman

Principal Commanders: Brig. Gen. George Crook
Forces Engaged: None
Casualties: None

A Brief on Fort Fetterman, located approximately eleven miles northwest of Douglas, Wyoming, is situated on a plateau above the valleys of LaPrele Creek and overlooking the North Platte River.

The fort was established as a military post on July 19, 1867, because of conditions that existed on the Northern Plains at the close of the Civil War. Civilization was advancing across the frontier along the line of the Union Pacific Railroad and the fort was needed as a major supply point for the army operating against the Indians. On July 31, 1867, the post was named Fort Fetterman in honor of Captain William J. Fetterman who was killed in a fight with Indians near Fort Phil Kearny, December 21, 1866. Major William McEnery Dye, with Companies A, C, H, and I, 4th Infantry, was assigned to build the post. Some of the buildings were from the North Platte Station later known as Fort Casper. In a letter to the Adjutant General, Major Dye described the post and surrounding country as ...situated on a plateau...above the valley of the Platte, being neither so low as to be seriously affected by the rains or snow; nor as high and unprotected as to suffer from the winter winds."[1]

Unfortunately, Major Dye's optimistic view of the site did not hold true for winter months. In November of 1867, Brigadier General H.W. Wessells became commanding officer at the fort. According to his report to the Department of the Platte, ..."officers and men, were found under canvas exposed on a bleak plain to violent and almost constant gales and very uncomfortable" the garrison managed to get through the winter. The fort continued to grow and develop until, by 1870, it was well established, and destined to play a conspicuous part in the Indians wars for the next few years. Jim Bridger, Wild Bill Hickock, Calamity Jane and "Buffalo Bill" Cody were among the colorful personalities of the time whose activities and travels took them frequently to Fort Fetterman and Fort Laramie.[1]

In accordance with the Treaty of 1868, Forts Reno, Phil Kearny, and C.F. Smith, along the Bozeman Trail were abandoned. Fort Fetterman, alone, remained on the fringe of the disputed area. As an outpost of civilization on the Western frontier, the fort represented protection and a haven to travelers.[1]

The fort was always considered a hardship post by officers and men who were stationed there. On May 18, 1874, Captain F. Van Vliet, of Company C, 3rd Cavalry, felt so strongly about the hardships on his men that he wrote to the Adjutant General requesting his company be transferred because there was "...no opportunity for procuring fresh vegetables, and gardens are a failure. There is no female society for enlisted men...the enlisted men of the company are leaving very much dissatisfied, as they look upon being held so long at this post as an unmerited punishment...whenever men get to the railroad there are some desertions caused by dread of returning to this post."[1]
Desertions were common, and the post frequently lacked adequate supplies and equipment. Supplies had to be hauled from Fort Laramie to the southeast or from Medicine Bow Station on the Union Pacific Railroad. Luxuries were scarce and pleasures few. However the soldiers found some diversion from the garrison life at a nearby establishment known as the "Hog Ranch."[1]

The "Famous Hog Ranch" was a bordello, and you can see it's location from the north end of the plateau, it is just across the bridge on Highway 93 on the left hand side. Currently, there is or was a newer trailer sitting on the land that once housed some of the best and only entertainment for the troops could enjoy away from the fort. Of course, the troops had to swim the river first to get there. My brother, Mark's noted, "at least they were clean when they arrived, he was sure that the soiled doves appreciated that".

During the mid-1870s, Fort Fetterman reached its pinnacle of importance when it became the jumping-off place for several major military expeditions. It was the base for three of General George Crook's Powder River Expeditions and Colonel Randall Mackenzie's campaign against Dull Knife and the Cheyenne Indians.

At the north end of the plateau look NE, across the river there is a huge flat field, this is the location Crooks' Camp that staged his troops waiting to begin his campaigns north against the hostiles.

With the resistance by the Indians resolved and confined to the reservations the fort outlived its usefulness and was abandoned in 1882, but it did not die immediately. A community grew up at the post and after 1882, it was an outfitting point for area ranchers and for wagon trains. The boom was short-lived, however, and in 1886, the town of Douglas was founded a short distance to the south. Most of the buildings were sold, dismantled or moved to other locations but as you walk around you can still see the building foundations.[1]

The visitors are welcome to walk the grounds where interpretive signs describe the Fort's buildings and activities. The reconstructed officers' quarters have maps, drawings, photographs, artifacts, and dioramas which interpret the history of the Indians, Military, and Civilians of Fort Fetterman and Fetterman City. The visitor is encouraged to walk the interpretive trail where signs describe the historic site and lead to a Gazebo overlooking Crook's Camp and the Indian Country to the north. The site provides several picnic areas and a shelter for group or individual use. Historic guided tours are available upon request and by appointment by calling Fort Phil Kearny State Historic Site (307) 684-7629.[1]

---

1. www.forttours.com/pages/tocftfetterman.asp

Chapter 14

Guernsey (Oregon-California Trail) Ruts & Register Cliff

Oregon Trail Ruts outside of Guernsey, WY [1]

Other Names: Pioneer Trail Ruts, Wagon Trail Ruts
Location: Three miles south of Guernsey, WY. Good Signage to the Ruts and large parking lot and to Register Cliff.
Campaign: None
Date: None
Principle Commanders: None
Forces Engaged: None
Casualties: None

The resulting ruts were cut into the soft sandstone by the iron rimed wagon wheels on the wagons. At this location the trail was forced away from the river and crosses a ridge of sandstone, the track is worn to a depth of five feet, creating some of the most spectacular ruts remaining along the entire length of the Oregon-California Trail. The geography of the area dictated that practically every wagon that went west crossed the ridge in exactly the same place, cutting the deep rut into the rock. You should walk up a slight incline to the ruts from the parking lot it is less than 100 yards, they are indeed impressive. Think while your standing in the center of the track or rut how many brave pioneer passed this way to settle our wonderful country.

Oregon-California Trail ruts outside Guernsey [1]

Close by the Trail Ruts is the famous Register Cliff State Historical Site. You will find interpretive signs as you walk around. This Cliff is soft sandstone verse the harder Granite at Independence Rock.

R. Kent Morgan

Register Cliff near Guernsey [1]

In Register Cliff parking lot:

GPS reading: 42° 14.842N X 104° 42.699W Elev. 4322
This is a beautiful spot and when I visited in the early morning there were lots of deer around so be careful driving. There is a cave that was cut into the bottom of the cliff by a local farmers to store; I believe potatoes and other perishables, because it kept them cool inside.

Historical Trivia:

As your driving southeast to Fort Laramie you will see a Historical Sign on Oregon Trail Rifle Pits, your left hand side of the road at:

GPS reading: 42° 16.038 N X 104° 47.424W, Elev. 4493.

This road Highway US26/85 follows the Oregon-California Trail and the sign indicates some old Rifle Pits dug along the trail. It is called the Cold Springs Campsite and is about 500" on the brow of the hill overlooking US26/85. I can't recall the reasoning for the rifle pits other than perhaps the pioneers saw Indians and decided to be on the defence as they settled in for the night?

---

1. www.wyonebtourism.com/NorthP/TrailRuts/

Chapter 15

Fort Laramie

"Old Bedlam," the original Post Officer's Quarters built in 1849, is the oldest documented standing structure in Wyoming. Fort Laramie preserves numerous original structures, with over 50 historically furnished rooms. [1]

Other Names: Fort William's, and Fort John

Location: Just south of the town of Fort Laramie, WY on US 26/85. well marked on the road signs. Good blacktop road out to the fort, and at the entrance,

GPS coordinates: 42° 12.323N X 104° 33.757W Elev. 4213

Campaign: Red Cloud War

R. Kent Morgan

Date: 1849-1890
Principle Commanders: Over a hundred Commanding Officers
Forces Engaged: None
Casualties: None

Originally the fort was built in 1834 and named Fort William's (later Fort John), this site was the first permanent trading post set up in what is now the State of Wyoming. Most of the great Indian treaties were signed there. All the pioneers stopped here to visit and re-supply or sell excess supplies, this is a very historic site on your adventures.
Just up the path from the large parking lot is a memorial to the Pony Express. As you face "Old Bedlam" to your far left would have been the site and foundations of the original Fort close to the river.

With the famous Treaty of 1868, a condition was that the white men were forbidden to enter the Powder River country, but prospectors made their way into the adjacent Black Hills which caused the Indians to protest by continued raids on settlements. The climax of Indian fighting came in 1876 when Generals Crook, Custer, Terry, Mackenzie, Miles, and great Chiefs Sitting Bull, Dull Knife, Red Cloud, Crazy Horse and others wrote American history with bullets and arrows. Driving the Indians to the reservations that we have today.

Fort Laramie as a post was abandoned in 1890. The site is under extensive restoration and the National Park Service is going a fantastic job in restoration.

This is a beautiful fort and several buildings are waiting for your visit. They all have period furnishing and the Army Barracks is outstanding. They have a wonderful Visitor Center with an excellent video as well as great souvenirs and a small museum. The rangers are there to help answer your questions. They are an excellent resource so we should utilize their expert knowledge.

Author (white t-shirt and brother Mark) standing before Ft. Laramie Cavalry Barracks

Historical Trivia:

Ordnance Sergeant Leodegar Schnyder
One of the least known but most significant figures in the history of Fort Laramie. Schnyder arrived at Fort Laramie with Company G, 6th U.S. Infantry, on August 12, 1849. He was appointed as assistant post librarian on September 17, 1851. Schnyder was promoted to the rank of Post Ordnance Sergeant on December 1, 1851. On September 17, 1859, he was appointed Garrison Postmaster, concurrent with his other duties. Despite requesting transfers on numerous occasions, Schnyder did not leave Fort Laramie until the fall of 1886. Schnyder retired in 1890. Ordnance Sergeant Schnyder holds the record for the longest term of service at Fort Laramie, 37 years, and is among the record holders for the longest term of service in the U.S. Army for an enlisted man—a total of 53 years. [1]

Wheat Flour (Ah-ho-ap-pa)

Ah-ho-ap-pa was the daughter of the Brule Chief Spotted Tail. Legend has it that she was enamored by the white way of life. She reputedly fell in love with an army officer at Fort Laramie, but was separated from him when he was transferred to another post. Apparently one of Ah-ho-ap-pa's favorite pastimes was watching the soldiers at formal dress parades. Although much of her life is a mystery, we do know that in keeping with his daughter's wishes, Spotted Tail brought her to Fort Laramie for burial. Colonel Henry Maynadier provided a military escort for the burial party and arranged to have a scaffold erected on the high ground overlooking the fort to the North. Maynadier issued orders to provide full military honors to the girl. After the tumultuous events of 1876, Spotted Tail retrieved his daughter's bones and took them to the reservation for reburial.[1]

John "Portuguese" Phillips Plaque

Just as you approach Fort Laramie there is a left hand 90° curve and right at that curve is a Plaque commemorating John "Portuguese" Philips famous ride from Fort Kearny to Fort Laramie in December 1866 to report the Fetterman's Massacre and to request reinforcements for Ft. Kearny.

Fort Laramie Military Bridge
Military Bridge photos courtesy Library of Congress, Prints and Photographs Division [1]

As you cross over the North Platte River you will see this Iron Bridge on your left hand side. Just beyond the bridge as I recall is a dirt road off to the right that takes you up on a hill side overlooking the fort on your left. There are a few spots where pioneers are buried. I don't remember all but ask at the fort about this ground one of the senior rangers can tell you.

---

1. www.ultimatewyoming.com
Another interesting web site is www.cr.nps.gov.

Chapter 16

Grattan Fight

Grattan Massacre Memorial Stone [1.]

Other Names: Grattan Massacre, Grattan Fight
Location: Drive through the town of Fort Laramie, go east 1 mile on US26/85, to the Pony Soldier RV Park (on your left hand side) and take a right turn at:
GPS Coordinates: 42° 10.703N X 104° 26.368W, Elev. 4215.
Directly across from the RV park is a nice blacktop county road that will cross over the RR tracks and follow this country road out for 4 miles. You will be heading south and then take a left hand curve and heading east about a mile or two, on your right you will see a historical sign denoting the Oregon Trail. Now drive slowly for another 1/5 of a mile and on the left hand side is a Stone Monument for the Grattan Fight.
GPS Coordinates: 42° 07.942N X 104° 24.347 W, Elev. 4201.

Actually, the Grattan Fight is located in the middle of the field on your left, facing the monument inscription. When I was there it was a corn field. I understood from one of the rangers at Ft. Laramie, there is a stone monument in the middle part of the field to mark the spot.
The Grattan Fight occurred some eight miles southeast of Fort Laramie.

Campaign: None
Date: August 19, 1854
Principle Commanders: Brevet 2nd Lieutenant John L. Grattan, Sixth U.S. Infantry

Chief Conquering Bear, Brule Sioux

Forces Engaged: 1 Officer, 29 Men and 1 Interpreter
    4,000 Indians

Estimated Casualties: 30 Troops killed and 1 Interpreter
    1 Indian (Chief Conquering Bear)

Brief Background:
In the late summer of 1854 about 4,000 Brule and Ogallala Sioux were camped near Fort Laramie in accordance with the terms of an earlier peace treaty. On August 17, 1854 a cow, belonging to a Mormon wagon train who was traveling on the Oregon Trail nearby, wandered into the Sioux camp, and the wayward cow was killed.

On August 19, 1854, Second Lieutenant Grattan an impetuous young officer of the Sixth U.S. Infantry was put in command of a detachment of 29 enlisted men and an interpreter and was sent to arrest the Indian for supposedly stealing and killing an Mormon emigrant's cow in a Brule Indian camp eight miles east of Fort Laramie.

It is unknown exactly what transpired at the Indian village, which contained approximately 4,000 Indians. Shots were fired mortally wounding Chief Conquering Bear and Grattan's 29 enlisted men, and the interpreter were killed. The enlisted men killed in this engagement are buried in Fort McPherson National Cemetery, near North Platte, Nebraska.[2] Most historians agree that this incident started the Indian Wars on the Plains. It is my understanding that a young Indian boy named, Curly witnessed this confrontation and would later grow up and be given the name of Crazy Horse a celebrated War Chief of the Sioux.

Aftermath of the Grattan Fight:

News of the massacre reached the War Department and plans were put in to motion for retaliation. General William S. Harney (actually recalled from a European Tour) commanded elements of his own 2nd Dragoons and units from the 6th and 10th Infantry and the 4th Artillery Regiments. His command set out on August 24, 1855 to find and extract revenge from the Sioux.

On September 3, 1855 on the Blue Water Creek, near Ash Hallow, just west of Ogallala, NE, Harney's 600 troops charged a camp of 250 Sioux men, women and children. Harney had declared days earlier "By God, I'm for battle -- no peace". It was with that he ordered his men to open fire on the community of Sioux. 85 Brules were killed, including some women and children. Afterwards the Army made a wide sweep of the surrounding Sioux country but encountered no further resistance. For his handling of the battle at Ash Hollow, Harney was known afterwards among the Sioux as "the Butcher."

Crazy Horse was but a child at the massacre and survived; he had a spiritual vision foretelling of his future as a warrior.

For military officials and the increasing numbers of emigrants traveling the Oregon Trail, the battle bought them 10 more years of relative peace.

---

1. www.americanindian.net/2003.html (Phil Konstantin's 2003 Vacation)
2. McDermott, A Guide to the Indian Wars of the West, p.190

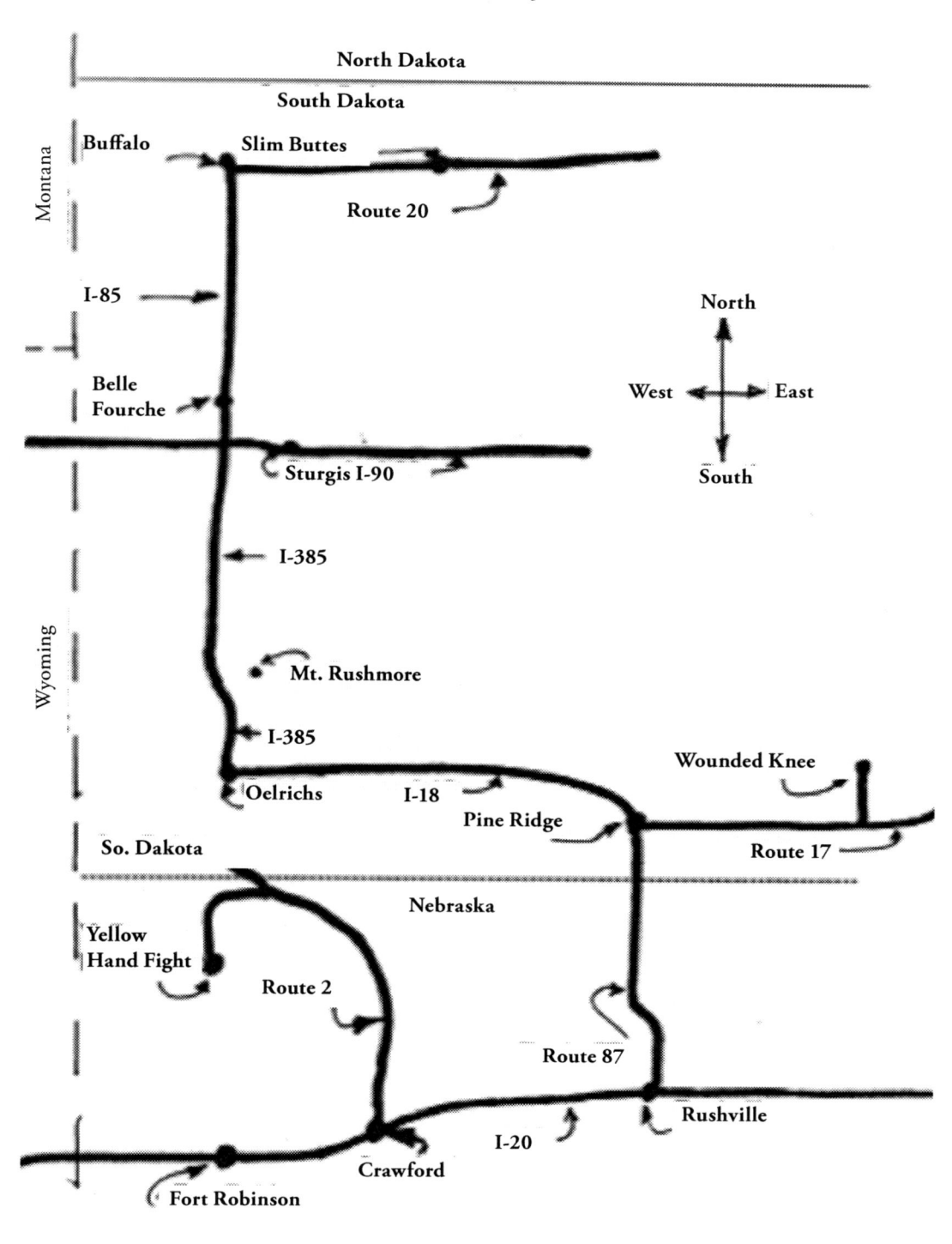

Guide Book To The Indian War Battlefields In Eastern WY, Neb. & SD

Chapter 17

Fort Robinson
Includes Sunrise Loop, Red Cloud Agency, spot where Crazy Horse was killed, the Northern Cheyenne barracks and German Prison of War Camp.

Pictures above are reproduction cabins at Fort Robinson, just in front of the cabin on the right is a rock monument indicating the place were Crazy Horse was killed as he struggled from being arrested. [1]

Other Names: Red Clouds Agency
Location: After seeing the Gratten Fight retrace your route back to US26/85 turn right as you cross the rail road tracks heading east. Drive to Lingle and take a left turn on Highway US 85 and drive up to Lusk, WY. At Lusk take US 20 and proceed east. Highway 20 cuts right through the Center of Fort Robinson

Campaigns: None
Date: 1874-1945
Principle Commanders: Several Post Commanders starting with General Crook
Forces Engaged: None
Estimated Casualties: None

Fort Robinson has several things to see. First as your traveling east on the left hand side is a large valley containing the Fort Robinson Buffalo herd (75 – 100 head) and you can see them from the highway. Great shaggy beasts that once occupied this area in the millions, not thousands but millions. How could one every think after seeing the huge herds that they would every be at the edge of extension.

Slow down and before crossing over Soldiers Creek there is a Historical sign:
GPS reading: 42o 39.186N X 106o 29.797 W Elev. 3851

This sign indicates the escape route of the Northern Cheyenne during their winter breakout from Fort Robinson in 1879. This loop takes you on a 40 minute driving tour with interpretive signs and puts you back on US 20. Take a left hand turn and drive back down to Fort Robinson, the loop is a beautiful drive.

R. Kent Morgan

Fort Robinson sign, the small stone monument over my brother's right shoulder is the spot where Crazy Horse was fatally wounded.

Upon crossing over Soldiers Creek to your right is the old portion of the fort where you will see three log cabin structures. There is a stone podium in front of one of the smaller cabins this is the spot where Crazy Horse was mortally wounded during his arrest.

Indicating where Crazy Horse was fatally wounded

Immediately in front of the log cabin buildings is a very large parade ground. The longer larger cabin was the location of the barracks that the Northern Cheyenne escaped from.

On your left side of the highway is the newer (late 1800's) portion of the fort. There at your first left turn is a beautiful two story Visitor Center this was the old barracks. Stop and see them and get a fort map. There is a nice restaurant in this building with lots of pictures and artifacts on both floors.

In March, 1874, the U.S. Government authorized the establishment of a military camp at the Red Cloud Agency on the White River. Once home of some 13,000 Indians, many of whom were hostile, the Agency was one of the most troublesome spots on the Plains. The camp was named Camp Robinson in honor of Lt. Levi H. Robinson, who had been killed by Indians the previous month. In May, the camp was relocated on this site, and in January, 1878, was officially designated Fort Robinson.

Fort Robinson played an important role in the Indian wars from 1876 to 1890. Crazy Horse surrendered here on May 6, 1877, and was fatally wounded that September while resisting imprisonment. In January, 1879, the Fort was the scene of a major battle as the result of the Cheyenne Outbreak led by Chief Dull Knife.

In the 20th Century, Fort Robinson became the world's largest military remount depot, and during the second World War, was the site of a K-9 corps training center, and German prisoner-of-war camp. The Fort's deactivation following the war marked the end of more than 70 years of service as Nebraska's "outpost on the plains."

R. Kent Morgan

Large parade ground is just in front of the Visitor Center/Hotel, the building in back of the soldiers standing is the Fort Museum [1]

Take a drive around the fort grounds and visit the museum there. It was a very active fort. At one time for just a few months General Douglas MacArthur's father Arthur MacArthur was posted here. The fort was home to both the 9th and 10th Cavalry "The Famous Buffalo Soldiers".[1]

Ask for directions to the Red Cloud Agency location, at the Visitor Center or consult your Fort map that you got at the Visitor Center.
The directions are: drive east from the visitor center slowly on Highway 20 and take a right turn on the east side of the Playhouse Theater at Fort Robinson. At the south side of the building there is a gravel road, drive on this road staying left and it will take you first to the location of the World War II German POW Camp (you can actually the building foundations). Staying on this gravel road it will loop around to the location of the Red Cloud's Agency there is a commemorative stone.

GPS Coordinates 42o 40.244N X 103o 26.203W, Elev. 3781

This is an immense area that would have been covered with thousands of TP's at one time, making up the following of Chief Red Cloud.

---

1. www.nebraskahistory.org

Chapter 18

Yellow Hand Fight

Monument Hill [1]

Montrose Community Church [1]

R. Kent Morgan

> SITE
> WHERE
> SEVEN COMPANIES OF THE FIFTH
> U.S. CAVALRY
> UNDER
> COL. WESLEY MERRITT
> INTERCEPTED 800 CHEYENNES
> AND SIOUX EN ROUTE TO JOIN
> INDIANS IN THE NORTH
> JULY 17, 1876
> THE CHEYENNES AND SIOUX WERE DRIVEN BACK TO
> THE RED CLOUD AND SPOTTED TAIL AGENCIES
> RECONSTRUCTED IN 1997 BY THE
> FRIENDS OF THE WARBONNET BATTLEFIELD

Plaque indicating where 5th Cavalry intercepted the Cheyenne and Sioux [1]

Other Names: Yellow Hair Fight, Skirimish at Warbonnet Creek, Warbonnet Creek Fight, Hat Creek Fight and later known as Fort Montrose

Location: From Highway 20 to from Ft. Robinson, to Crawford, take Highway 71 north or to South Dakota border. From Crawford, NE to the county road off Highway 71 & 2 is 27.7 miles.

GPS coordinates: 43° 00.052N X 103° 38.510W Elev. 3630. This reading is taken off Highway 71 & 2.

NOTE: DO NOT CROSS SOUTH DAKOTA BORDER
Note: Exist off Highway 71 on the left traveling North, just 300 yards or so from the South Dakota border.

The battlefield is 9.8 miles off the highway on a gravel road. This exist off the highway takes you down a slight hill to a railroad crossing and on the left side you will see the sign "Hat Creek Road"

GPS coordinates: 42° 59.445N X 103° 38.497W Elev. 3665

Continue straight across over the R/R tracks and continue on 9.8 miles on Hat Creek Road.

You will see the Montrose County Church on your left side, directly across from church at:

GPS coordinates: 42° 55.367N X 103° 43.787W Elev. 3705
is the entrance to the Yellow Hand Battlefield and you will see two Memorials to your right: One is the Battlefield memorial on a small hill:

GPS coordinates: 42° 55.636N X 103° 43.738W Elev. 3751

and another memorial (closer to the road) is the spot where Buffalo Bill killed Yellow Hand:

GPS coordinates: 42° 55.403N X 103° 43.673 W Elev. 3683

Campaign: Meeting General Crook's Column for the Yellowstone Expedition
Date: July 17, 1876
Principal Commanders: Col. Wesley Merritt and Lt. Col. Eugene A. Carr

    Chief Lone Wolf of the Cheyenne

Forces Engaged: 200 Troopers of the 5th Cavalry
    800 Cheyenne

Casualties: None for the Cavalry
    1 for the Indians a Chief Yellow Hand of the Cheyenne

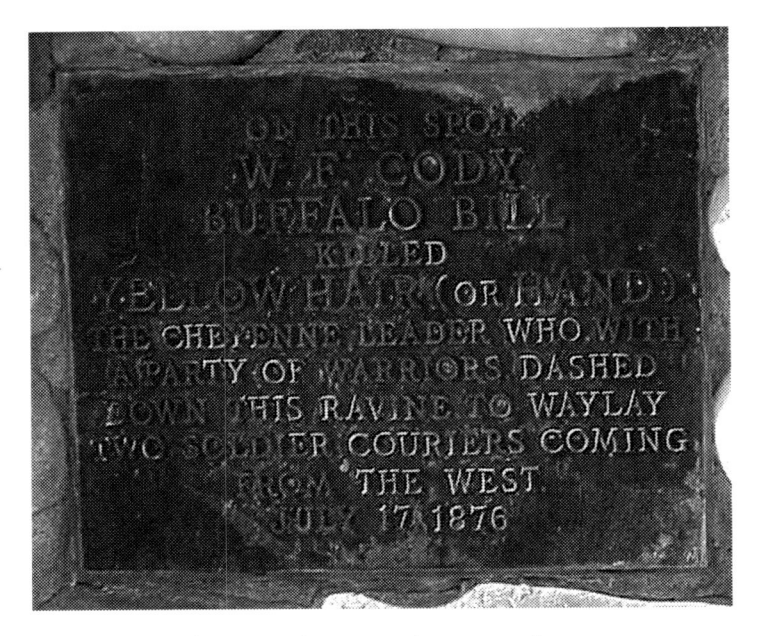

Plaque indicating the spot where
Buffalo Bill killed
Chief Yellow Hand (or Hair) [1]

Buffalo Bill Cody (William F. Cody) passed through Fort Laramie in 1876, while en route north with the Fifth Cavalry. Cody was a well known frontiersman, Pony Express rider, buffalo hunter, scout, and showman. Shortly after passing through Fort Laramie Cody had his famous duel with Yellow Hair at the War Bonnet Creek Fight on July 17th, 1876. Cody took Yellow Hair's scalp—an event widely touted as "the first scalp for Custer."

After the defeat of Custer at the Little Big Horn, many Native Americans joined with Sitting Bull and Crazy Horse encouraged by the Indians' success. About 800 Cheyenne warriors set out from the Spotted Tail and Red Cloud agencies in Nebraska.

The Army was also receiving reinforcements. Col. Wesley Merritt, commanding the 5th Cavalry, had set out to join with Gen. George Crook in Montana, guided by the legendary "Buffalo Bill" Cody.

Merritt was able to intercept the Cheyenne warriors before he reached Crook. Merritt planned an ambush. The veteran cavalry officer hid most of his 200 troopers inside covered wagons and posted sharpshooters nearby but out of sight.

Spotting Merritt's seemingly unescorted wagon train along Warbonnet Creek, the Cheyenne warriors charged directly into the trap. A few warriors were wounded by the troopers, but the only real action of the engagement was a duel between "Buffalo Bill" and a young warrior named Hay-o-wei (translated as Yellow Hair). Cody pulled his Winchester carbine and killed the Indian, then pulled out a Bowie knife and scalped the dead man. The rest of the warriors under Chief Lone Wolf broke and fled so quickly that not a single trooper was killed or injured. Merritt was able to join with Crook, who in turn linked up with General Alfred H. Terry, bringing a combined strength of the U.S. force to about 4,000.

A scout accompanying the cavalry misidentified the dead Indian as the important Cheyenne Chief Yellow Hand. Ever the showman, Buffalo Bill returned to the stage in October, his show highlighted by a melodramatic reenactment of his duel with the supposed Yellow Hand. He displayed the fallen warrior's scalp, feather war bonnet, knife, saddle and other personal effects. The warrior's scalp, war bonnet, knife, pistol and other personal effect can still be seen in the Buffalo Bill Museum in Cody, Wyoming.

Historical Trivia:

After the Indian wars, settlers moved in a set up ranch on this land. When the Ghost Dancers Religion was on the rise and word of Wounded Knee in 1890 at Pine Ridge reached the settlers, they quickly organized and immediately built a temporary defense that consisted of a circular trench around the top of the hill denoting the site where Merritt's men were stationed. The settlers also dug an underground chamber at the bottom of the hill. The dubbed this Fort Montrose. [2]

While your driving east on Highway 20 and passing the town of Chadron, NE about a mile out of town is the "Museum of the Fur Trade" on your right hand side. They have a fantastic collection of firearms and other items used in the Fur Trade, well worth your while, to stop and see as your passing through.

---

1. www.americanindian.net.2003.html
2. www.genocites.com/naforts/ne.html
Another reference is the book Hedren, Paul L., "First Scalp for Custer"

Chapter 19

Wounded Knee

Wounded Knee Battlefield Sign [1]

Other Names: Wounded Knee, Indian name Cankpe Opi

Location: From Crawford, NE drive east on US 20 to city limits of Rushville, then take a left turn on to Highway 87 to Pine Ridge.
At the stop light take a right turn on Highway 18 proceed for 9 miles to a large green sign with an arrow pointing north to Wounded Knee 7 miles on Route 27.

Approximately 150 yards off Highway 18, on Route 27 there is a huge interpretive sign for Crazy Horse. Note: The number of bullet holes in the sign.

GPS coordinates at Crazy Horse Sign:
43° 02.860N X 102° 22.619W, Elev. 3418

At 7 miles there is a Y in the road follow Route 27 to the right. You will see another huge interpretive sign for the site of Massacre of Wounded Knee. GPS coordinates at Wounded Knee Sign:

43° 08.467N X 102° 21.758W, Elev. 3222

Campaign: Pine Ridge Campaign, associated with Ghost Dance Spiritual movement
Date: December 29, 1890
Principal Commander: Col. James W. Forsyth, CO of 7th Cavalry

Chief Big Foot of the Sioux
Forces Engaged: 500 Troopers
350 Indians

Casualties: 25 Troopers killed and 39 wounded
153 Indians killed and 50 wounded

Preface: The Ghost Dance
In 1888, a Piute Holy Man named "Wovoka" in Nevada developed new spiritual movement that if the Indians danced, meditated and chanted

they would bring back the traditional way of life, the dead would be resurrected, they would see great herds of buffalo, and there would be no whites to contend with. This became known as the Ghost Dance Religion or Movement.

Government officials were becoming alarmed with the new religious fervor and in December 1890 banned the Ghost Dance on Lakota reservations. When Ghost Dance continued they called in the Army to suppress it on Pine Ridge and Rosebud Reservations in South Dakota.

The presence of additional troops created great tension with the current situation. The dancers sent word for Sitting Bull to join them. Before he could set out from the Standing Rock reservation in North Dakota, he was arrested by Indian police. A scuffle ensued in which Sitting Bull and seven of his warriors were slain. Six of the policemen were killed. Chief Big Foot and his followers had already departed south to Pine Ridge, asked there by Red Cloud and other supporters of the whites, in an effort to bring tranquility. General Nelson A. Miles sent out the 7th Calvary led by Major Whitside to locate the Chief Big Foots following. The Calvary located the tribe 30 miles east of Pine Ridge. The Indians offered no resistance. Big Foot, ill with pneumonia, rode in a wagon. The soldiers ordered the Indians to set up camp five miles westward, at Wounded Knee Creek.

The Battle:
Colonel James Forsyth arrived to take command and ordered his guards to place four Hotchkiss cannons on a hill overlooking the Indian camp. The soldiers now numbered around 500; the Indians 350, all but 120 of these women and children.[1]

The following morning, December 29, 1890, the soldiers entered the camp demanding that all Indian firearms be relinquished. A scuffle between a soldier and Indian ensued a firearm was discharged. The silence of the morning was broken and soon other guns echoed in the river bed. At first, the struggle was fought at close quarters, but when the Indians ran to take cover, the Hotchkiss artillery opened up on them, cutting down men, women, children, and with sick who Big Foot was among. By the end of this unnecessary violence, which lasted less than an hour, at least 150 Indians had been killed and 50 wounded. In comparison, army casualties were 25 killed and 39 wounded (killed and wounded by fire from their own troops or friendly fire). General Nelson Miles preferred charges against Col. Forsyth for the killing women and children but the colonel won exoneration. [2]

Trooper among the dead Indians at Wounded Knee [2]

Note: The Hotchkiss guns were placed some 300 yards SW of the Wounded Knee Sign. It would have been located on Cemetery Hill. Directly across from the sign on the hill is a cemetery with a crumbling red brick arch with an iron cross on top. At the cemetery there is a 4 foot tall marble monument erected in the middle of the fenced area. This is the final resting place of Chief Big Foot and over 250 of his followers. There are 46 warriors' names on the monument itself.
GPS reading at cemetery entrance: 43° 08.535N X 102o 21.888W, Elev. 3287

As you face the cemetery entrance on the right side, there is a visitor center down the hill.

Medal of Honor - Recipients

Sergeant William Austin, Cavalry, directed fire at Indians in ravine.
Private Mosheim Feaster, Cavalry, extraordinary gallantry
Private Mathew Hamilton, Cavalry, bravery in action
Private Joshua Hartzog, Artillery, rescuing commanding officer who was wounded and carried him out of range of hostile guns
Private Marvin Hillock, Cavalry, distinguished bravery
Sergeant Bernhard Jetter, Cavalry, distinguished bravery for "killing an Indian who was in the act of killing a wounded man of B Troop."
Sergeant George Loyd, Cavalry, bravery, especially after having been severely wounded through the lung.
Sergeant Albert McMillain, Cavalry, while engaged with Indians concealed in a ravine, he assisted the men on the skirmish line, directed their fire, encouraged them by example, and used every effort to dislodge the enemy.
Private Thomas Sullivan, Cavalry, conspicuous bravery in action against Indians concealed in a ravine.
First Sergeant Jacob Trautman, Cavalry, killed a hostile Indian at close quarters, and, although entitled to retirement from service, remained until the end of the campaign.
Sergeant James Ward, Cavalry, continued to fight after being severely wounded. Corporal William Wilson, Cavalry, bravery in Sioux Campaign, 1890
Private Hermann Ziegner, Cavalry, conspicuous bravery.
Corporal Paul H. Weinert, the gunner from Company E, 1st U.S. Artillery, taking the place of his commanding officer who had fallen severely wounded, he gallantly served his place, after each firing he advanced the artillery to a better position.
Private George Hobday, Cavalry, was given a Medal of Honor for conspicuous and gallant conduct in battle.
First Sergeant Frederick Toy, Cavalry, was given a Medal for voluntarily bringing water to the wounded soldiers under fire.
Musician John Clancy, U.S. Artillery was awarded a Medal of Honor for twice voluntarily rescuing wounded comrades under fire of the enemy.
2nd Lt. Harry Hawthorne, Artillery, also received a Medal for distinguished conduct in battle with hostile Indians.

First LT. Ernest Garlington, Cavalry, awarded for distinguished gallantry. First Lt. John Gresham, Cavalry, for voluntarily leading party into ravine to dislodge Sioux Indians concealed therein, and was wounded during the action.

Historical Trivia: The day after the Battle of Wounded Knee on December 30, 1890 there was a skirmish between the Sioux and the 7th Calvary at White Clay Creek near Drexel Mission. I understand this site is a couple of miles north of Pine Ridge, you would have to ask at Big Bats (a large convenience store at the main stop light at junction of Highway 87 and US 18). During this skirmish one trooper was killed and Lieutenant James Defrees Mann was seriously wounded and later died at Fort Riley, Kansas on Jan. 15, 1891, plus 6 other troopers were wounded during this action. The number of Indians killed and wounded is unknown.

While skirmishing with the Sioux, Captain Charles Varnum of Company B, First Sergeant Theodore Ragnar of Company K, Farrier Richard Nolan of Company I, were awarded the Congressional Medal of Honor for bravery.

Captain Charles Varnum, graduated from West Point in 1872. He distinguished himself while executing an order to withdraw, seeing that a continuance of the movement would expose another troop of his regiment to being cut off and surrounded. Varnum disregarded orders to retire, placed himself in front of his men, led a charge upon the advancing Indians, regained a commanding position that had just been vacated, and thus insured a safe withdrawal of both detachments without further losses and saved countless lives.

Grave Site of Chief Red Cloud is at the Native American Cemetery, Oglala just 15 miles NW of Pine Ridge on Highway 18.

---

1. www.americanindian.net/2003/476.jpg
2. www.lastoftheindependents.com/wounded.htm
www.etsu.edu/cas/history/docs/miles.htm (Statement by Gen. Miles on Wounded Knee)
Another website www.en.wikipedia.org

Chapter 20
Slim Buttes Battlefield

The Slim Butte Monument
The battlefield would be the high hill in the distance.

Other Names:
Location: Location is on Highway 20, from Buffalo, SD driving east 23 miles. When you pass the Custer National Forest which contains some incredible rock formations, you're getting close to the Slim Buttes Monument. Actually just past the Custer National Forest driving east, will see high hills on the right side. These are parts of the Slim Buttes battle site.

R. Kent Morgan

At GPS coordinates 45º 32.611N X 103º 37.486W, Elev. 3145. is the Slim Buttes Battle Site Monument

The monument is only 50 ft. or so off the highway sitting on a knoll. Interpretive signs are around the monument and the view to the battlefield. The actual battlefield is about half a mile away from the monument looking SW. For another view point, drive east another 1/5 of a mile and turn right on to Highway 79 and drive down a ¼ mile to:

GPS coordinates 45º 32.280N X 103º 05.682W, Elev. 3082
You can look west 240º compass heading for eastern view of the battlefield.

Campaign:
Date: September 9-10, 1876
Principle Commanders: Captain Anson Mills, Third Cavalry
    Chief American Horse
Forces Engaged: 150 Troopers from 3rd Cavalry
    100 Warriors and 300 women and children
Casualties: 3 Troops were killed
    5 Indians were killed

Slim Buttes looking South the village would be located on the left hand side.

Following the Little Bighorn debacle, Generals Alfred Terry and George Crook took up an unsuccessful summer chase of the Sioux. As the campaign continued into Fall, Gen. Crook's column found itself out of supplies and near starving. Crook ordered part of the column under

Capt. Anson Mills to strike out and reach the Black Hills to find supplies during which his command accidentally stumbled onto Chief American Horse's village on the evening of September 8, 1876, near the present town of Reva, South Dakota. Mills' Third Cavalry troopers surrounded the village and attacked it the next morning. Taken by surprise, the village was destroyed and Chief American Horse fatally wounded and died later in the evening.[1] Other assaults during the Fall and Winter convinced most of the Sioux and Cheyenne of the futility of fighting the soldiers. The site currently resides on private land.

The three troopers that were killed were attempting to drive warriors including Chief American Horse out of concealment in a ravine.

Later during the day Crook brought up the rest of the command and they bivouacked at the Slim Buttes and were re-supplied with captured Indian's winter supplies. The Indians continued harassing fire on the troops until they vacated the site and continued their trek to the Black Hill. Crook upon leaving buried his dead on the battlefield.

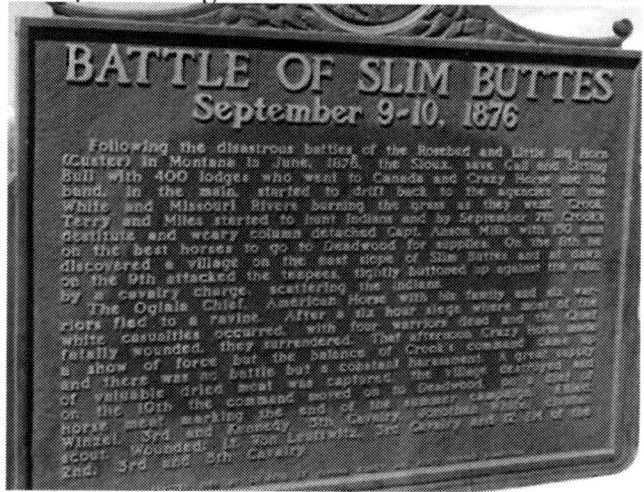

Sergeant John A. Kirkwood, Company M, 3rd Cavalry, awarded the Medal of Honor for Battle of Slim Buttes for Bravely endeavored to dislodge some Sioux Indians secreted in a ravine.

---

1.   www.nps.gov/foda/Fort Davis
Good Book - Greene, Jerome A., Slim Buttes 1876

Appendix #1 – Medal of Honor

The Medal of Honor awarded
during the Indian Wars [1]

The readers might ask themselves why so many Medals of Honor were awarded?

My explanation is as follows; The Medal of Honor was basically the only medal that could be awarded to both enlisted and officers during these Indian Wars.

The Medal of Honor (Army) was first authorized by Congress on July 12, 1862, and was the same as the Navy Medal, authorized a few months earlier with a different suspension. There were 1,520 medals awarded during the Civil War. There were 428 medals awarded during the Indian Wars, all to the Army. Six were awarded posthumously.

The criteria for the Medal of Honor at this time were simply valorous conduct on the field of battle. Most of the 31 Medals awarded to the 5th Infantry under Colonel Nelson Miles simply read: "Gallantry in Engagement or Gallantry in Action".

Having said this, there was another medal that could have been awarded to enlisted personnel (Privates only) called the Certificate of Merit.

Certificate of Merit [2]

The Certificate of Merit was established during the Mexican War by an Act of Congress of March 3, 1847, Medal 1905 and discontinued July 9, 1918, it was originally a Paper Certificate, to be awarded by the President to Privates only for gallantry in action, or for special meritorious service in time of peace. Some 545 men received the Certificates of Merit during the Mexican War. It wasn't until January 11, 1905, that a medal was authorized to be worn. Due to the Certificate of Merit limitations it was not awarded in the Indian Wars, leaving only the Medal of Honor.

During the Indian Wars from 1865 to 1891, which commenced immediately following the Civil War, the U.S. Army was engaged in a series of small battles with the Indians over a number of years.

These were from skirmishes to a few pitched battles, but did not compare to the magnitude seen during the Civil War.

For the most part, the Officers and NCOs were combat hardened veterans of the Civil War. The ranks were filled mostly with new immigrants, some of whom had fought in the Civil War. Most joined because of the economic conditions following the Civil War. The Indians called them either Horse Soldiers or Long Knives (Cavalry) or Walk-a-Heaps (Infantry).

Troops were engaged throughout this period, yet the Indian's Campaigns were third page news until June 25, 1876, when tragic news of Battle at the Little Bighorn became front page news.

Congress did not recognize the Indian Wars until March 1890, when they recognized the troops as "Veterans" in a sense that they campaigned against an armed enemy of the United States.

1. www.wikipedia.org/wiki/Congressional_Medal_of_Honor
2. www.medal.org.uk/usa

Appendix # 2 – Indian War Medal

**Indian War Campaign Medal
from Author's collection**

The War Department General Order No. 12 established Indian Wars Medal on January 21, 1907 some 42 years after the Indian Wars began.

The Indian Campaign Medals were awarded for military service against any tribes or in any areas listed below during 1865 to 1891: The ribbon is Red with two vertical Blue strips on each side; the face of the medal has a mounted Indian Chief with a lance. Indian Wars is cast above the

Indian. On the reverse is cast the American Eagle with United State Army above the Eagle and For Service cast under the Eagle.

Indian Campaigns as follows:

- Southern Oregon, Idaho, Northern California, and Nevada between 1865 to 1875.
- Comanche's and confederated tribes in Kansas, Colorado, Texas, New Mexico, and Indian Territory between 1867 to 1875.
- Modoc War (Northern California, and Southern Oregon) 1872 to 1873.
- Apaches in Arizona in 1873.
- Northern Cheyenne and Sioux in 1876 to 1877.
- Nez Perce War in 1877.
- Bannock War in 1878.
- Northern Cheyenne in 1878 to 1879.
- Sheep-Eaters, Piutes, and Bannocks between June and October 1879
- Utes in Colorado and Utah between September 1879 and November 1880
- Apaches in Arizona and New Mexico in 1885 to January 1891.
- Sioux in South Dakota between November 1890 to January 1891.

Appendix #3 - Biographies Of The Officers, Troopers And Chiefs

What became of these Officers, Troopers and Chiefs and other notables that were directly involved in the Indian wars?

President Ulysses Simpson Grant, (1822–1885), President (1869-77), Civil War Lt. General, and West Point graduate. After the presidency entered business on Wall Street and lost all his money. Wrote magazine articles about his military life, diagnosed with throat cancer in 1884, wrote his autobiography and finished it right before his death. The sales from the book restored his family's wealth. Buried at General Grant National Memorial, New York City.[1]

Lieutenant General William Tecumseh Sherman, (1820-1891), Civil War Lt. General and West Point graduate. Known for his march through Georgia to the sea during the Civil War. Became General of the Army after the Civil War during Grant's Administration. Buried at Calvary Cemetery, St. Louis, Missouri.[1]

Major General Philip Henry Sheridan Sr., (1831-1888) died in Chicago. Civil War Major General and West Point graduate. Promoted to Lt. General of the Army, who replaced William T. Sherman after retirement. Died suddenly of a heart attack while on duty. Buried at Arlington National Cemetery.[1]

Brigadier General George Crook, (1830-1890) died in Chicago, Illinois. West Point graduate and Major General in command of the Department of the Missouri. Promoted Lt. General of the Army, died of a heart attack in Chicago. Buried at Arlington National Cemetery.[1]

Brigadier General Alfred H. Terry, (1832-1890), Harvard graduate, promoted to Major Gen. in 1886, Commander of the Missouri, retired on disability 1888. Buried at Grove Street Burial Ground, Hew Haven, CT.

Brigadier Patrick Edward Connor, (1820-1891), born around Killarny, Ireland. Immigrated to USA with parents, enlisted in Army to fight in the Seminole Wars 1839, Mexican Wars 1846 serving as a Captain of volunteers. Traveled to California to be a miner, commissioned Colonel in 1861 and ordered to Utah where he established Fort Douglas. Fought and defeated the Shoshone Indians at Bear River

1-29-1863, promoted to Brig. Gen. Lead the Power River Expedition against hostile Sioux, Cheyenne, and Arapaho who had been disruptive on the Bozeman Trail. After this campaign he was brevetted to Major Gen. and discharged at the end of the Civil War. He went back into mining founding the first silver mine in Utah (Known as the Father of Mining in Utah) and started first newspaper in Salt Lake. He founded a city named Stockton in honor of his California Militia. He died on 12-17-1891 and is buried at Fort Douglas Cemetery in Salt Lake City.[1]

Major General William Selby Harney, (1800-1889), received a commission in 1818. He distinguished himself in the Florida Campaigns against the Creeks and Seminoles and rapidly attained promotions, becoming a Lt. Colonel by 1836. By 1846 just prior to war with Mexico he was promoted to Colonel. This promotion placed him as one of the Senior Colonels under General Winfield Scott in the advance to Mexico City. Scott distrusted his judgment and relieved him of command. Scott was overruled by President James K. Polk, who had been a neighbor to the Harney family in Tennessee, and he quickly vindicated his reputation by his gallant conduct at Gerro Gordo, for which he received the brevet of Brigadier General on April, 1847.

From the end of the Mexican War to Civil War he put down Indian uprisings. As a result of the Grattan Fight, he led the Battle of Ash Hollow in 1855 were he was both cursed and praised for his actions. It was from this battle that the Indians called him "The Butcher"-his troops killing some 250 men, women and children of the Brule Sioux. He then spent some time on the Great Plains helping negotiate treaties with several tribes. He was one of the commissioners that met at Ft. Laramie in 1868 to negotiate the treaty that ended the Red Cloud War.

He was promoted to Brig. General in Regular Army in June, 1858. At the beginning of the Civil War he was one of four General Officers in the Army. The others were Brevet Lieutenant General Winfield Scott, Brig. General John E. Wool, and Edwin V. Summer.

His family was allied strongly with the pro-Southern elements and during the Civil War he tried to keep Missouri out of the war Washington authority reviewed this with suspicion and he was relieved of command and saw no service in the war. He retired in 1863 and at the close of the war he was brevetted to Major General. He died in Orlando, Fl. 5-9-1899 and is buried at Arlington National Cemetery.[1]

Grenville Mullen Dodge, (1831-1916), worked on the railroad, graduated from Norwich University in Civil Engineering and raised an Iowa Regiment for the Civil War, commissioned Colonel of the Iowa Volunteers. Appointed Brig. General for leadership at the Battle of Pea Ridge and placed in command of the District of Mississippi protecting and building railroads. In 1864 appointed Major General and engaged at Battle of Ezra Church and wounded in the knee. He was appointed to command Dept. of the Missouri. It was during this period he ordered a punitive campaign to quell these raids along the Bozeman Trail. This command was given to Brig. Gen. Patrick Edward Connor, who commanded the District of Utah. Connor's men inflicted a decisive defeat on the Arapaho Indians at the Battle of the Tongue River, but the expedition in general was inconclusive and eventually escalated into Red Cloud's War.

Dodge retired at the end of the war, and elected the US congress and after one term retired from politics and returned to railroading engineering. He became Chief Engineer of the Union Pacific and led the construction for the Transcontinental Railroad.

The famed Western frontier town Dodge City, Kansas, was named in his honor. Dodge Street in Omaha, Nebraska, the former location of Union Pacific Headquarters is also named for him.

Dodge went to New York City to manage his growing number of businesses he had developed. He returned to his home and died and is buried at Walnut Hill Cemetery, Council Bluffs, Iowa. [1]

General Henry Walton Wessells, (1809-1889), he graduated from West Point in 1833 and served in the Seminole and Mexican wars. During the Civil War Wessells was wounded and named Brig. Gen. of Volunteers in 1862. After the war he was brevetted Brig. Gen. in regular army which he remained and served in the West as a Colonel relieved Col. Henry B. Carrington at Fort Kearny in January, 1867 and he retired in 1871, died at home in Dover, Delaware on 1-12-1869 and buried in Arlington Nat. Cemetery.[1]

Colonel Ranald Slidell Mackenzie, (1840-1889). Ranald Slidell ("Bad Hand", or "Three-fingers") Mackenzie, graduated from the US Military Academy in 1862 first in his class of 28. Commissioned 2nd Lt. fought in the Civil War for 3 years in eight major battles, received seven brevetted promotions and six wounds, had two fingers shoot off during the battle of Petersburg campaign. During his final campaign against Robert E. Lee, he was a brevetted Major General at the age of 24 (know as one of the "Boy Generals"). At Appomattox he took custody of surrendered Confederate property and afterward commanded the cavalry in the Department of Virginia.

In 1867, Mackenzie accepted an appointment as colonel of the Forty-first Infantry. In 1871-75, he assumed command of the Fourth United States Cavalry and ended the Red River Wars in the south west.

After Custer's troops had been annihilated on the Little Bighorn River in 1876, Mackenzie was placed in command of the District of the Black Hills and of Camp Robinson, Nebraska. In October he forced Sioux Chief Red Cloud, who had won a campaign in 1868 against the United States, to return his band to the reservation. On November 25 Mackenzie decisively defeated the Northern Cheyennes. After a short tour of duty in Washington, during which he commanded troops mustered to keep the peace in the event of disturbances following the presidential election of 1876, Mackenzie returned to the Black Hills, then to Fort Sill. In late 1877 Indians from Mexico were again raiding in South Texas, and by March 1878 Mackenzie was again at Fort Clark. He began patrols and in June led an expedition into Mexico. His incursion prompted the Mexican government to act, and by October the raiding had ceased.

In October 1879, he put don the Ute uprising. On September 2, 1881, he was ordered to subdue the Apaches. In October 30, 1881 he took command of the District of New Mexico. He was promoted to the rank of brigadier general, but was seriously ill. On October 27, 1883, he was reassigned to command the Department of Texas. He planned to marry and retire on land that he had bought near Boerne, TX.

In December 1883, he was suffering "paralysis of the insane." He was sent to New York City and placed in the Bloomingdale Asylum. On March 24, 1884, he was retired from the army. In 1886 he was moved to New Brighton, Staten Island, where he died on January 19, 1889. He was buried at West Point Military Academy Cemetery, NY. [1]

Colonel James William Forsyth, (1836-1906), attended West Point. After serving in Washington Territory at Fort Bellingham and Camp Pickett, San Juan Island, Forsyth was promoted to Lt. in 1861 and returned to the East to command Union forces in the Civil War. Became Chief of Staff for Major General Philip H. Sheridan. He took part in military campaigns against the Comanche, Cheyenne, Arapaho, and Kiowa Indians in 1868-69. Forsyth commanded cavalry units in the 1878 Bannock campaign, and in succeeding years, spent most of his time inspecting cavalry units throughout the West. He was promoted to colonel in 1886 and placed in command of the 7th Cavalry stationed at Fort Riley, Kansas. In December 1890, Forsyth led his troops to the Pine Ridge Agency in South Dakota. On December 29, in the midst of mounting tension, Forsyth's attempt to disarm the Indians turned into a fight, later known as the Wounded Knee massacre. On the following day, Forsyth again engaged the Indians at Drexel Mission. Forsyth's actions were investigated at General Miles' instigation, and although he was cleared of any wrongdoing, Forsyth resented Miles' accusations.

Forsyth was commissioned brigadier general in December 1894 and appointed commander of the Department of California. He served in this position until his promotion to Major General in May 1897 when he retired from the military.

In 1867 James Forsyth married the daughter of the governor of Ohio, William Dennison. She died around 1888. By 1877, the couple had four children: a son, William Dennison Forsyth, who also entered the military, Marion, Betsy, who married Dallas Bache, a career military officer, and a fourth child. On retirement, Forsyth moved back to his native Ohio. He died on October 24, 1906 and is buried at Greenlawn Cemetery in Columbus, Ohio.[1]

Colonel Nelson Cole, (1833-1899). He recruited a company of volunteers in April, 1861 and was commissioned a Captain of Volunteers. In 1863 he was assigned to the Artillery, promoted to Major after the surrender of Vicksburg and promoted Colonel in 1864. In July, 1865 his command proceeded on the Powder River Expedition to support Gen. Patrick Connor command. Mustered out in November, 1865 and continued in the business. During the Spanish-American he was commissioned Brig. Gen. l but given only home duty. Died on 7-31-1899 St. Louis and buried in the Bellefontaine Cemetery, St. Louis, MO.[1]

Colonel Henry Beebee Carrington, (1824-1912). Educated at Yale after 1861 made his career in the military. On 5-4-1861 was appointed Colonel of the 18th Infantry, on 11-29-1862 promoted to Brigadier General. Carrington's duties during the War included organizing and sending 120,000 Indiana volunteers to the front. After the Civil War,

Carrington opened a wagon route to Montana through Wyoming. He constructed Fort Phil Kearney and fought off attacks by area Sioux. Relieved of command in early Jan, 1867 and retired from the Military in 1870 spending the rest of his life trying to vindicate himself. Carrington's wife Margaret, whom he had two sons, died in 1870, but he remarried the following year to the widow Frances Grummond whose husband Lt. George Washington Grummond was killed with Capt. Fetterman in Dec., 1866. He taught military history at Wabash College for a number of years. He died on Oct. 26, 1912, and is buried at Fairview Cemetery, Hyde Park, MA.[1]

Colonel Wesley Merritt, (1834-1910), One of the boy Major Generals during the Civil War. Graduated from West Point in 1860, served in Utah in the cavalry. Had a distinguished career during the Civil war at wars end with rank of Lt. Col. in regular army. Commanded the 5th Cavalry during the Indian wars. He was in command of the 5th Cavalry at the Yellow Hand Fight with Wild Bill was his Chief of Scouts driving the Indians back to their reservation. Was appointed Superintendent of West Point from 1882-1887 and appointed a Brigadier General in the regular army. He commanded the VIII Corps and was military governor of Manila during the Spanish-American War. Promoted to Major General in 1895. Merritt retired from the Army in 1900 and died ten years later in Natural Bridge, Virginia. He is buried in Arlington National Cemetery.[1]

Lt. Colonel Eugene Asa Carr, (1830—1910), Educated at West Point graduating in 1850, ranked 19 in class of 44, served in the southwest fighting Kiowa and Comanches. During Civil War, promoted Colonel, wounded 3 times, awarded Medal of Honor for gallant leadership during the battle at Elkhorn Tavern. After the war he returned to the frontier to fight Plains Indians. Promoted to Brig. General in 1892. He retired in 1893 and spent his later years supporting the National Geographic Society. Carr died in Washington, D.C. in 1910 and is buried at West Point Cemetery.[1]

Lt. Colonel William O. Collins, died 1880). He was commissioned Lt. Col. in his 1st Independent Battalion Ohio Volunteer Cavalry and discharged in April, 1865 after service in the West. He, his wife Catherine and two daughters made their home in Hillsboro, Ohio which is still standing. After his discharge, this lawyer, railroad president and later State Senator learned that his only son, 20-year-old 1st Lt. Caspar Collins, who had been under his command on the North Platte River, died in a skirmish with Indians while trying to rescue a wagon train on July 26 west of the Platte Bridge Station in the Dakota Territory. He and his son left a permanent mark on the west Casper, WY was named after his son and Fort Collins, Colo., took its name from William. He died in 1880 and is buried with his family in Greenwood Cemetery in Hillsboro, Ohio.1

Major Frank Joshua North, (1840-1885), brother of Luther North, worked as a clerk in the Trader's store at the Pawnee Agency in 1856. He learned the Pawnee language and became an interpreter.

In 1864 the Army employed him to organize and lead a company of Pawnee Scouts; in 1865 he was commissioned a Captain. In 1865, he and his scouts saw action under Gen. Patrick Conner, following this action; the Pawnee gave him the name "Pani Le-Shar", (Chief of the Pawnee) as a special tribute. He saw action with Gen. E. A. Carr in, 1869. North was promoted to Major and served under Gen. George Crook and Col. Ranald Mackenzie in 1876-77. Led the Pawnee's at the Dull Knife Battle.

After 1877 he retired from the Army, served as State House of Representatives in 1882-83. He, with Buffalo Bill Cody and his brother Luther North actively managed a ranch. He performed with Buffalo Bill's "Wild West" Show. He was considered the best revolver shot on the Plains. Frank North died in his home on March 14, 1885 and is buried in Columbus, Nebraska. He was named to the Cowboy Hall of Fame in Okalahoma City in 1958.[1]

Captain Luther Hedden North, (1846-1935), brother of Frank North, worked as a mail carrier, cowboy and enlisted in 1862 with Columbus 2nd Cavalry in Co. "K" the regiment was assigned guard duty against the Sioux. He fought under Gen. Sully in 1863. After 1864 he hauled freight from Omaha to Columbus. In 1866 he went to Michigan where he attended school. In 1867, his older brother Frank recruited him as Captain to lead the Company "D" First Battalion Indian Scouts. He participated in several skirmishes including the Dull Knife Battle.

North retired from the Army 1877, was engaged in the cattle business with his brother and W.F. Cody. In 1882 he returned to Columbus and bought and sold horses and cattle. During the following years he was a deputy internal revenue collector, worked in the livestock business, was a farmer, and storekeeper for the Gov't. in Omaha. He married in 1898 went to California, returned to Columbus became a blacksmith, farmer and also had a store. He outlived his famous bother Major Frank North by a half century. Luther North died April 19, 1935 in his home and is buried in Columbus, Nebraska.[1]

Captain Anson Mills, (1834-1917), Attended West Point from 1855-57, but did not graduate. Engaged in land surveys and engineering projects in Texas, where he laid out the first plans for the city of El Paso. He left Texas in 1861 in order to volunteer for the Union Army. Was appointed to the 3rd US Cavalry. Participated in the Indian Wars and commanded US troops at the battle of Slim Buttes, Dakota, September 9, 1876. Invented the woven cartridge belt for the Military and became very wealthy. He was promoted to Brig. General in 1893 and retired. He was a member of the Mexican Boundary Commission. He is buried at Arlington National Cemetery.[1]

Lieutenant Charles Albert Varnum, (1849-1936), West Point Graduate class of 1868, assigned to 7th Cavalry in 1876, Chief of Scouts and last officer to speak with Custer at the Little Big Horn and fought with Major Reno and Capt. Benteen. Awarded Medal of Honor in 1897 during a skirmish at White Clay Creek near Pine Ridge in 1890, he disregarded orders to retreat when he noticed another regiment about to be surrounded and he led his company to support the other regiment 's withdraw whereby saving countless lives. He was promoted Captain, 1897, Major in 1900, Lt. Colonel in 1901, and retired Colonel in 1919. He is buried at San Francisco National Cemetery in California.[1]

Lieutenant Caspar Collins, (1845-1865), son of the Post Commander, William 0. Collins, and officer of the 11th Ohio Volunteer Cavalry. Collins left detailed accounts of life at Fort Laramie during the Civil War period. Unfortunately for young Collins, he became most well-known in death. On July 25, 1865, Collins led a group of 25 soldiers out of Platte River Bridge Station to relieve a detachment of ten soldiers guarding a supply train that was approaching the station. Indians closed in on the soldiers; Collins' horse bolted and ran into the group of Sioux. Collins and four other soldiers were killed. Platte River Bridge Station was soon renamed Fort Caspar. His remains were shipped home and buried at Greenwood Cemetery in Hillsboro, Ohio.[1]

Lieutenant James Defrees Mann, (Died 1891). Graduated from West Point in 1873, assigned to Seventh Cavalry June, 1877, promote to First Lieutenant July, 1890, received serious wounds in action with Sioux at White Clay Creek, South Dakota, near Drexel Mission, Pine Ridge along with 6 other troopers, on Dec. 30, 1890 a day after Wounded Knee Battle. Lt. Mann died of his wounds at Fort Riley, Kansas and is buried at Arlington National Cemetery.[1]

Lieutenant John Gregory Bourke, (1846-1894), Bourke's career as a soldier began in 1862. At the age of 16, he enlisted as a private with the 15th Pennsylvania Cavalry on August 12. Bourke's first battle as a soldier took place at the Battle of Stone River, Tennessee, in January of 1863. Awarded the Medal of Honor for Gallantry in Action during Battle of Murfreesboro, TN in Dec. 1862. On July 5, 1865, his remarkable intelligence earned him an appointment to West Point Academy as a cadet. He began to study to be an author on October 17, 1865, and he also graduated on June 15, 1869, 4th in his class of 39. One year later Bourke was assigned to Third Cavalry promoted to Captain. Bourke would remain in this Calvary until his death on June 8, 1894, nearly 27 years later. Through his military career, Bourke began to keep journals concerning events and personalities as a form of personal record of his experiences in the Old West. He is buried in Arlington National Cemetery.[1]

Second Lieutenant John l. Grattan, (died 1854), graduated from West Point. First and last command at Fort Laramie killed in skirmish with Indians August 19, 1854. Buried first at Ft. Laramie, then at Ft. McPherson (his command of 22 men are buried there) and Lt. Grattan was re-interred at Ft. Leavenworth National Cemetery, Kansas.[1]

Private James Bell – MEDAL OF HONOR RECIPIENT

Rank and organization: Private, Company E, 7th U.S. Infantry. Place and date: At Big Horn, Mont., 9 July 1875. Birth: Ireland. Date of issue: 2 December 1876. Citation: carrying dispatches to Gen. Crook at the imminent risk of his life. He rose to rank of Sergeant, died in July, 1901 and is buried at Mount Olivet Cemetery, Chicago, IL.[2]

Private William Evans – MEDAL OF HONOR RECIPIENT

Rank and organization: Private, Company E, 7th U.S. Infantry. Place and date: At Big Horn, Mont., 9 July 1876. Entered service at: St. Louis, Mo. Birth: Ireland. Date of issue: 2 December 1876. Citation: Carried dispatches to Brig. Gen. Crook through a country occupied by Sioux. He died in August, 1881 and is buried at Bellefontaine Cemetery, St. Louis, MO.[2]

Private Benjamin F. Stewart – MEDAL OF HONOR RECIPIENT

Rank and organization: Private, Company E, 7th U.S. Infantry. Place and date: At Big Horn River, Mont., 9 July 1876. Birth: Norfolk, Va. Date of issue: 2 December 1876. Citation: Carried dispatches to Gen. Crook at imminent risk of his life.[2]

First Sergeant Thomas H. Forsyth - MEDAL OF HONOR RECIPIENT

(1843-1908) First Sergeant, Company M, 4th U.S. Cavalry. His citation read: "Though dangerously wounded, he maintained his ground with a small party against a largely superior force after his commanding officer had been shot down during a sudden attack and rescued that officer and a comrade from the enemy".

Sergeant Forsyth typified the best of the old-line noncoms—intelligent, conscientious, faithful, seasoned by long experience, and devoted to the Army. Enlisting in 1861 at the age of 18, he served in an Ohio Volunteer regiment through 4 years of Civil War and after Appomattox joined the Regular Army. As first sergeant of Troop M, 4th Cavalry, he fought hostile Indians from Texas to Montana. When the regiment attacked the Cheyenne camp of Dull Knife in Wyoming on November 25, 1876, Forsyth's troop commander, Lt. John A. McKinney, went down with mortal wounds. With two other noncoms, the first sergeant protected the body from charging warriors intent upon a scalp. A bullet wound in the temple sustained here, together with another in the spine received in the Civil War, and would plague Forsyth the rest of his life. Fifteen years later, on July 14, 1891, he was awarded a Congressional Medal of Honor "for distinguished gallantry" in this engagement.

Appointment to staff duty was one means a rewarding outstanding noncommissioned officers, and on the recommendation of his regimental commander, Col. Ranald S. Mackenzie, Forsyth received such a post. Throughout most of the 1880's he served as commissary sergeant at Fort Davis, and here he and his wife, who had followed him from one outpost to another since 1871, reared their eight children. On December 20, 1898, in his eighth enlistment, Sergeant Forsyth retired from the Army after 37 years of service. He died in San Diego on March 22, 1908 and is buried at Mt. Hope Cemetery in San Diego.[2]

Sergeant George Grant, MEDAL OF HONOR RECIPIENT

Sergeant Grant was with "F" Company, 18th US Infantry, he was awarded his medal for his bravery in a journey between Fort Phil Kearny to Fort C.F. Smith, Dakota Territory in February 1867. His citation reads "Bravery, energy, and perseverance, involving much suffering and privation through attacks by hostile Indians, deep snow etc., while voluntarily carrying dispatches". His medal award on May 9, 1871. Sgt.

Grant died on Sept. 1, 1876 and is buried at Arborville Rural Cemetery at Stockville, Nebraska.[2]

MEDAL OF HONOR - RECIPIENTS from Battle of Wounded Knee[2]

Sergeant William Austin, Cavalry, directed fire at Indians in ravine, died July 1929, cremated at Cypress Lawn Memorial Park, California. Private Mosheim Feaster, Cavalry, extraordinary gallantry, rose to 1st Lt. died March 1950 buried at Golden Gate National Cemetery, California

Private Mathew Hamilton, Cavalry, bravery in action

Private Joshua Hartzog, Artillery, rescuing commanding officer who was wounded and carried him out of range of hostile guns. Rose to rank of Sergeant, died May 1939 buried at Gum Springs Cemetery, Searcy, AK.

Private Marvin Hillock, Cavalry, distinguished bravery

Sergeant Bernhard Jetter, Cavalry, distinguished bravery for "killing an Indian who was in the act of killing a wounded man of B Troop." Rose to 1st Sgt., died Aug. 1927, buried Cypress Hills National Cemetery, Brooklyn, NY.

Sergeant George Loyd, Cavalry, bravery, especially after having been severely wounded through the lung. Rose to 1st Sgt., committed suicide on Dec. 1892, buried at Fort Riley Post Cemetery, Fort Riley, KS.

Sergeant Albert McMillain, Cavalry, while engaged with Indians concealed in a ravine, he assisted the men on the skirmish line, directed their fire, encouraged them by example, and used every effort to dislodge the enemy. Died Oct. 1948, buried at Oakland Cemetery, St. Paul, MN.

Private Thomas Sullivan, Cavalry, conspicuous bravery in action against Indians concealed in a ravine. Died Jan. 1940, buried Holy Sepulchre Cemetery, East Orange, NJ.

First Sergeant Jacob Trautman, Cavalry, killed a hostile Indian at close quarters, and, although entitled to retirement from service, remained to close of the campaign. Retired from Army, died Nov. 1898, buried South Side Cemetery, Carrick, PA.

Sergeant James Ward, Cavalry, continued to fight after being severely wounded. Died Mar. 1901, buried New Calvary Cemetery, Mattapan, MA.

Corporal William Wilson, Cavalry, bravery in Sioux Campaign, 1890. Died Jan.1928, buried Rosehill Cemetery, Hagerstown, MD.

Private Hermann Ziegner, Cavalry, conspicuous bravery.

Corporal Paul H. Weinert, the gunner from Company E, 1st U.S. Artillery, taking the place of his commanding officer who had fallen severely wounded, he gallantly served his place, after each fire advancing it to a better position.

Private George Hobday, Cavalry, was given a Medal of Honor for conspicuous and gallant conduct in battle. Enlisted several times in Infantry and Cavalry units, died Dec. 1891, buried Jefferson Barracks Nat. Cemetery, St. Louis, MO.

First Sergeant Frederick Toy, Cavalry, was given a Medal for voluntarily bringing water to the wounded soldiers under fire. Rose to Captain, died Aug. 1933, buried at Riverside Cemetery, Lewiston, NY.

Musician John Clancy, U.S. Artillery was awarded a Medal of Honor for twice voluntarily rescuing wounded comrades under fire of the enemy. Rose to 1st Sgt., died July, 1932, buried at Fort Riley Post Cemetery, Fort Riley, KS.

2nd Lt. Harry Hawthorne, Artillery, also received a Medal for distinguished conduct in battle with hostile Indians. Rose to the rank of Colonel, died Apr. 1948, buried at Arlington National Cemetery.
First Lt. Ernest Garlington, Cavalry, awarded for distinguished gallantry. Rose to the rank of Brig. General, died Oct. 1934 buried at Arlington National Cemetery.

First Lt. John Gresham, Cavalry, for voluntarily leading party into ravine to dislodge Sioux Indians concealed therein, and was wounded during the action. [2] Died Sep. 1926, buried San Francisco National Cemetery, San Francisco, CA.

Sergeant John A. Kirkwood – MEDAL OF HONOR RECIPIENT

Rank and Organization: Sergeant, Company M, 3d U.S. Cavalry. Place and Date: At Slim Buttes, Dakota Territory, 9 September 1876. Birth: Allegheny City, Pa. Date of Issue: 16 October 1877. Sergeant, Company M, 3d U.S. Cavalry. Place and Date: At Slim Buttes, Dakota Territory, 9 September 1876. Birth: Allegheny City, Pa. Date of Issue: 16 October 1877. Citation: Bravely endeavored to dislodge some Sioux Indians secreted in a ravine. Died in 1930, buried Soldier Home National Cemetery, Washington, DC.[2]

Sergeant Charles L. Thomas – MEDAL OF HONOR RECIPIENT

Born 2-12-1843, Died 2-24-1923 during the Powder River Indian expedition in Wyoming in the fall of 1865, Captain Humpfervill returned to the camp of General Connor of the 11th Ohio Cavalry after a scout of 300 men, to report that Colonel Cole of the Regiment was surrounded by Indians near the Powder River. General Conner called for a volunteer "to go as a scout and find Cole or perish in the attempt." (C.L. Thomas) Sergeant Charles Thomas volunteered and spent 36 hours traveling about 201 miles alone in hostile territory to find Colonel Cole and deliver a message from General Conner. After leaving Conner's camp at 8 A.M., on his second day, Sergeant Thomas was sighted by hostile Indians in the area as he followed Colonel Cole's trail, and "began to exchange shots - and it was a running fight for the balance of the day." Capturing an Indian pony, Thomas kept it with him in case his own horse was shot. During the day he stumbled across John Hutson of the 2d Missouri, who had become detached from Cole's element and was in hiding. Thomas had Hutson mount the spare pony, delivering him to Colonel Cole's camp after arriving about 6 P.M. to deliver the general's message.

Charles Thomas was commissioned a Brevet-Major, Ohio National Guard and entered on a special state Roll of Honor on February 18, 1921.[1]
Medal earned during the Indian Campaigns for Heroism September 17, 1865 at Powder River Expedition, Dakota Territory. Buried at Dwight-Morris Cemetery, Dwight, KS.

Frank Grouard, Chief of Scouts for Gen. George Crook (1850-1905), born a Polynesian and raised by a Morman family, as a young man he was captured by the Sioux and raised as an adopted son of Chief Sitting Bull. Excellent, Army Scout for General Crook in all the campaigns with the Sioux and Cheyenne. Buried at Ashland Cemetery, St. Joseph, MO.[1]

The following officers fought the majority of the time in Montana.

Colonel Nelson A. Miles, Born 8-8-1839, Died 5-15-1925, One of the boy Major Generals in Civil War, awarded Medal of Honor for gallantry at Chancellorsville during the Civil War. After war demoted to Colonel, promoted to Brig. Gen. 1880, promoted to Maj. Gen. in 1890 replaced Gen. John M. Schofield as Army's Command-in-Chief 10-5-1895, promoted to Lt. Gen. in 1901. Took mandatory retirement in 1903. Died of a heart attack while standing during the National Anthem with his grandchildren at a circus. Buried at Arlington National Cemetery.[1]

Colonel Elwell Stephen Otis, Born 3-25-1838, Died 10-21-1909, lawyer before the Civil War. Fought in the Indian War with Col. Miles. Promoted to Major General on June 16, 1906, led troops in the Spanish

American War and became Military Governor of the Philippine Islands from 1898 to 1900. Buried at Arlington National Cemetery.[1]

Colonel William Babcock Hazen, Born 9-27-1830, Died 1-16-1887, West Point graduate, Commander at Fort Buford during 1876 and 1877 Indian Wars. Later appointed by President Hayes a Chief Signal Officer as a Brig. Gen. buried at Arlington National Cemetery.[1]

Lt. Colonel George A. Custer, Born 12-5-1839, Died 6-25-1876, West Point graduate, last in his class. One of the boy Major Generals in Civil War due to his heroism. After the war he was reverted back to Lt. Colonel. Commanded the 7th Cavalry and died at Little Bighorn. He and his wife are buried at West Point Military Academy, NY.[1]

Major Marcus A. Reno, Born 11-15-1834, Died 4-1-89, West Point graduate, promoted to Brig. Gen. in Civil War. Led a column at the Battle of the Little Big Horn and survived. Later dismissed from Army for "prejudicial to the good order and discipline" and died on 4-1-1889 in Washington, DC. Re-interred in Custer National Cemetery in Montana in 1967 he is the highest ranking officer in the cemetery. [1]

Captain Frederick W. Benteen, Born 8-24-1834, Died 6-22-1898, Civil War Veteran. Participated in Battle of the Little Big Horn with Maj. Reno. Rose to the rank of Brig. General in 1890. Died in Atlanta and is buried at Arlington National Cemetery.[1]

Captain Thomas Benton Weir, Born 9-28-1838, Died 12-9-1876, graduated from University of Michigan in 1861, Civil War Veteran, served with the 7th Cavalry assigned to Major Reno's command at Little Bighorn. He attempted to rescue Custer, but was turned back by the Indians. His furthest point of advance is noted as "Weir's Point" at Little Big Horn Battlefield. He died in New York City, buried at Cypress Hills National Cemetery, Brooklyn, NY.[1]

Captain Simon Snyder, served in the 5th Infantry almost continuously from 1861 to 1888. He participated in the Fort Peck Expedition and later headed the mounted infantry detachment organized toward the end of the Sioux War. After a career spanning the Civil, Indian, and Spanish-American Wars, he retired as a Brigadier General in 1902. His diaries are an excellent and important resource.[1]

Captain Edmond Butler, Born 9-19-1827, Died 8-24-1895, received the Medal of Honor on 11-27-94, citation reads "Most Distinguished Gallantry in action against Hostile Indians" for his efforts on January 18, 1877 at the Battle of Wolf Mountain. He rose to the rank of Lt. Colonel. Died in Omaha, buried Holy Sepulcher Cemetery, Omaha, Nebraska.[1]

Captain James S. Casey, Born Philadelphia, Pennsylvania, received Medal of Honor for 1-18-1877 Battle of Wolf Mountain. Medal was issued and he was promoted to Colonel on the same day 11-27-1895 and commander of the 22nd Infantry from January 1895 – January 1897.[1]

Lieutenant Frank D. Baldwin, Born 6-26-1842, Died 4-22-1923, awarded Medal of Honor in Civil War and Second Medal of Honor in Indian Wars for rescuing two captive girls. Baldwin was under Col. Miles command during the Indian Wars. Fought in Spanish-American War. Promoted to Brigadier General in 1902. Retired from active duty 6-26-1906. Promoted to Major General in 1915. Died in Denver, buried at Arlington National Cemetery, about 40 yards away from Gen. Nelson A. Miles.[1]

Lieutenant George W. Baird, Born 12-13-1839, Died 11-28-1906, Medal of Honor recipient and received Medal in 1894, Citation reads, "Most distinguished gallantry in action with Nez Perce Indians". He was Col. Miles' Adjutant (from 1871 to 1879). He was severely wounded at the Bear Paw Mountains on 9-30-1877. Baird rose from a private during the Civil War to Brigadier General. He published accounts of Miles' campaigns and several officers. In 1879 he transferred to the Pay Department because of the wound received at Bear Paw, and retired in 1903. Buried at Milford Cemetery, Milford, New Haven County, Connecticut.[1]

Lieutenant Mason Carter, Born 1834, Died 1909 Civil War veteran and Medal of Honor recipient as a First LT. leading a charge under fire during the Nez Perce Indian Campaigns at Bear Paw Mountain in 1877. He rose to the rank of Major in the Army. Died in California and buried at Fort Rosecrans National Cemetery in California. He was the first Medal of Honor recipient to be interred in this cemetery.[1]

First Lieutenant Robert McDonald, Born 5-12-1822, Died 5-20-1901, received Medal of Honor for January 18, 1877 Battle of Wolf Mountain. Medal was issued on 11-27-1894. Died in Alameda County, CA, buried Lone Tree Cemetery, Hayward, California.[1]

Second Lieutenant James Worden Pope, Born 6-6-1846, Died 8-23-1919, West Point graduate of 1868, wrote eyewitness account of the Cedar Creek battle. At Wolf Mts. Battle commanded two artillery pieces. Later commanded U.S. Military Prison at Fort Leavenworth and as Chief Quartermaster of the expeditionary force to the Philippines in 1898. Pope retired as a Brigadier General in 1916 and died in Denver. Buried at Arlington National Cemetery[1]

Most of the Officers that died at the Little Bighorn are buried at Fort Leavenworth, Kansas. They include Keogh, Tom Custer, Yates, Smith, Calhoun, Harrington, Crittenden, Porter, Sturgis and Dr. Lord. Lt. Cook is buried in Hamilton Cemetery, Ontario, Canada.

Noted Native Americans Chiefs

Chief Red Cloud, Indian Name Makhpiya-Luta (1822-1909) He was a renowned Oglala Warrior and a Statesman.

In 1866 under Red Cloud's leadership conducted the most successful war against the United States by any Indian Nation. His strategies were so successful that the US agreed to the Treaty of 1868 at Ft. Laramie to abandon it's Bozeman Trail Forts and guarantee the Lakota their possession of what is now the western half of So. Dakota, including the Sacred Black Hills, and much of Montana and Wyoming.

Red Cloud agreed to live on the Pine Ridge Indian Reservation and promote peace with the whites.

He died of natural causes in 1909 and is buried at the Pine Ridge Cemetery.[1]

Chief Spotted Tail, Indian Name: Sinte Gleska (1823-1881) Noted Warrior and Brule Chief, during last 25 years of his life a proponent of nonviolent resolution with the dominant white population, while still insisting on retention of traditional culture.

When he was 30 he was chosen as a War Leader. It was Spotted Tail that led the warriors to attack and killed Lt. John L. Grattan and 20 troopers after attacking the Brule Village (better known as the Grattan Massacre) over a Mormon cow that was killed, thus starting the Indian Wars in 1854.

When Gold was discovered in the Black Hills the Gov't. wanted to buy this 150 miles by 50 miles volcanic mountain range for $400,000. Spotted Tail insisted that the Gov't. should buy for $60 Million so his people would live off the interest. Gov't. rejected Spotted Tail figure.

On August 5, 1881, Spotted Tail was returning from a Council meeting and was shot by another Indian. The motive for the murder seemed to be the jealously over the leadership.

A small monument was erected over his grave in the Rosebud Agency Cemetery. A more significant memorial was created in the form of a tribal college, now Sinte Gleske University on the Rosebud Sioux Reservation.[1]

Chief American Horse, Indian Name: Iron Shield, (1840-1876) He was an Oglala Sioux leader in Red Cloud's War in the 1860s and 1870s which fought to control the Bozeman Trail. American Horse, Crazy Horse, Young-Man-Afraid-of-His Horse and Sword were all made "Shirt-Wearers" in a ceremony in 1865. The Shirt-Wearers were essentially the leaders of the tribe.

With the discovery of gold in Montana and ignoring those Indian treaties of the 1850's. John M. Bozeman blazed a trail to the Montana Gold fields through Lakota hunting ground in 1862. In 1863 and 1864 he led settlers and miners across the trail despite attacks from the Indians trying to protect their hunting ground.

The gov't. ordered forts built along the Bozeman Trail. In December, 1866 American Horse led by Red Cloud fought a battle with a brash young Captain William J. Fetterman and 80 soldiers they were ambushed and all killed. This became known as Fetterman's Massacre.

Two years later the Peace Treaty of 1868 was signed at Fort Laramie by Red Cloud. The forts along the Bozeman Trail were burned down. American Horse elected to not live on a Reservation as Red Cloud did but to follow their traditional hunting of the buffalo.

American Horse and his band participated in the Battle at the Little Big Horn. On September 9, 1876, Captain Anson Mills accidentally discovered American Horse's camp at Slim Buttes and attacked at daybreak. American Horse was wounded and died that night. Ten Indians died, half were women and children and 3 soldiers died and another 20 wounded. Chief American Horse was probably buried in or around Slim Buttes.

Chief Dull Knife, Indian Name: Morning Star (1810-1883), As a Northern Cheyenne he participated in the Arapaho War in Colorado, the Sioux war for the Northern Plains and also the War for the Black Hills.

He participated in the defeat of Capt. John L. Fetterman and men outside Fort Kearny in 1866.

Dull Knife was away from camp during The Battle of the Little Big Horn. One of his sons participated and was killed during the Battle.

The pivotal battle of the Northern Cheyenne's occurred the early morning of the November 25, 1876, when Col. Ronald Mackenzie's force of 600 men of the 4th Cavalry and 400 Indian scouts surprised Dull Knife's camp on the Red Forks of the Powder River. The dead numbered around 40 but the destruction of the village and contents sealed their fate. The Northern Cheyenne surrendered to the General Crook and Mackenzie in the spring of 1877.

He is best remembered for leading his people back to Montana from their exile in Okalahoma in 1878. After being recaptured and placed at Ft. Robinson, NE the gov't. decided to send them back to Okalahoma. The Cheyenne tried to escape but were caught and pinned down in an oblong depression about 40 miles from Ft. Robinson resulting in the deaths of 23. Dull Knife and the remaining few, escaped to Pine Ridge Sioux Reservation and were hidden by the Sioux. They were eventually allowed to settle at the Northern Cheyenne Reservation at Lame Deer, MT.

He was married to 4 wives with whom they had 7 daughters and 4 sons.[1]
Chief Dull Knife died in 1883 at his son Bull Hump's home. He was re-interred along side of Little Wolf in the Lame Deer Cemetery in 1917.

Chief Little Wolf (1820-1904), He was a leader of the Northern Cheyenne. He, the Sioux and Arapaho warriors fought together in the War for the Bozeman Trail, better known as the Red Cloud War from 1866 to 1868. Little Wolf signed the Treaty of 1868 at Ft. Laramie.

In 1876 he was chief in the War for the Black Hills under Sitting Bull's leadership.
He was not a participant at the Battle of the Little Big Horn. He and Chief Dull Knife, led his people out of the reservation in Okalahoma in 1878. The group split in Nebraska and Little Wolf's ban surrendered to the Army in March, 1879. They were kept on the Pine Ridge Reservation with the Sioux until reunited on a New Northern Cheyenne Reservation in 1884 at Lame Deer, MT.

Little Wolf is buried beside Dull Knife at the Lame Deer Cemetery, Lame Deer, MT. [1]

Chief Gall, Indian Name Pizi (1840-1894) A noted Hunkpapa Chief who played a leading part in the Indian War against the US. He rose to prominence in the Red Cloud Campaigns. Gall became Sitting Bull's Military Chief. His family was killed by Reno's attack at the Little Big Horn. Gall lead the counter attack on Major Reno and drove him back to a defensive position on the hill. Gall and his warriors attacked and assisted in annihilating the troops with Col. Custer.

Gall fled with Sitting Bull to Canada and surrendered on Jan. 3, 1881 at Standing Rock Reservation. He championed efforts in farming and educational programs for the Lakota people. In 1889 he became a Reservation Court of Indian Offenses Judge. Chief Gall died on Dec. 5, 1894 at his home on Oak Creek in South Dakota.

Chief Plenty Coups, Indian Name Alaxchiaahust (Bull That Goes Against The Wind) (1848-1932). A noted Crow chief who allied the tribe very early with the US Gov't. to fight their noted enemy, the Sioux. Plenty Coup was a scout and fought with General George Crook at the Rosebud Battle in June 17, 1876 just 8 days before Battle at the Little Big Horn.

Chief Plenty Coups advocated a policy of cooperation and adaptation to the whites. He fought to preserve his peoples control over the land, resources and lives. He proved himself to be a strong and intelligent leader advocating education and self sufficiency. He was married about 12 times and had two children that both died young.

He was chosen by the Gov't. to represent all Native Americans at the dedication and burial of the First Unknown Soldier from WWI in 1921. He placed a wreath of flowers, his war bonnet and his coup stick at the tomb. He also spoke a prayer before the casket was lowered into its tomb.

He died March 4, 1931 and is buried with his two wives at the Plenty Coups State Park near Pryor, MT just south of Billings.[1]

Chief Rain-in-the-Face, Indian Name: Iromagaja, Iromagaju, Amarazhu, (1835-1905). He was a veteran of many battles against the military. He fought with Red Cloud in 1866 at "The Battle of Hundred Slain" now known as Fetterman's Massacre just north of Buffalo, WY.

He participated in the Battle of Little Big Horn. He is allegedly took the life of Tom Custer during the battle and after cutting out his heart, ate it. This has not been proven and during an interview in later life he indicated this was not true.

He fled with Sitting Bull to Canada and surrendered during the winter of 1880 at Fort Keogh (Miles City, MT). He spent his remaining life at Stand Rock Reservation in South Dakota and died on Sept. 14, 1905 and is buried near Aberdeen, SD.[1]

Chief Crazy Horse, Indian Name: Tashunca-uitco (1849-1877) He is celebrated as an Oglala Warrior and committed to preserving the traditions and values of the Lakota people.

Made a "Shirt-Wearer" in an 1865 Ceremony. He fought with Red Cloud to defeat Capt. John L. Fetterman outside Fort Kearny in 1866. He and American Horse followed the buffalo after The Treaty of 1868 at Ft. Laramie.

He participated and lead warriors at both the Battle of the Rosebud against General George Crook column, and at the Battle of the Little Big Horn, defeating the 7th Cavalry.

Was harassed by Col. Nelson A. Miles throughout the winter of 1876-77. Crazy Horse surrendered in May 1877 at Red Cloud Agency. In September 1877 General Crook ordered him arrested and while being incarcerated, he struggled and was bayoneted and died at Fort Robinson.

His body was taken by his father and buried around the Wounded Knee area at an unknown location.[1]

Chief Sitting Bull, Indian Name: Tatanka-Iyotanka (1831-1890), a Hunkpapa Lakota Chief and Holy man under whom the Sioux and other tribes united in their struggle for survival on the northern plains. Sitting Bull remained defiant until the end toward the military power and contemptuous of Gov't. promises to the end.

After a Sun Dance just north of Lame Deer, MT he had a vision of the soldiers falling upside down in to his village. He was foreseeing the Battle of the Little Big Horn and the defeat of the 7th Calvary. Sitting Bull was present at the Battle but did not participate because of his weakened condition from the Sun Dance.

During the Fall and Winter of 1876-77 after being harassed by Col. Nelson A. Miles and Lt. Frank D. Baldwin troops at Cedar Creek, MT and Ash Creek, MT (about 45 miles North of Terry, MT) Sitting Bull took a small contingent of his people to Canada.

Sitting Bull surrendered at Ft. Buford, MT on July 19, 1881. He was sent to Ft. Randall for 2 years as a prisoner of war. In May, 1883 he settled at the Standing Rock Reservation where he lived in a cabin refusing to give up his old ways as the reservation rules required. He did send his children to a nearby Christian school believing that the next generation of Sioux needed to read and write for the future.

In the fall of 1890, the creation of a Ghost Dance started and this ceremony promised that the land would be rid of white people and restore the Indians old ways. The reservation authorities feared that Sitting Bull as a spiritual leader would promote this and cause trouble. The authorities sent 43 reservation police to bring him in, but during the arrest and struggle with his followers outside his cabin a gunfight followed, with one of the policemen shooting Sitting Bull in the head. Sitting Bull is buried at Mobridge, SD where a granite shaft marks his grave. [1]

Chief Big Foot, Indian Name: Si Tanka (Spotted Elk) (1825-1890) He became a chief of the Minneconjou in 1874, which is one of the seven subdivisions of the Teton Sioux. The Minneconjou were present at the Battle of the Little Big Horn.

After the Indian Plain Wars the Minneconjou was placed on the Cheyenne River Reservation in South Dakota.

With the Ghost Dance Religion movement in practice and the hearing of Sitting Bull's death, Big Foot decided to move his Minneconjou tribe to settle in with the Pine Ridge Reservation and was intercepted by an army detachment on Dec. 28, 1890. They camped at the Wounded Knee Creek. On the morning of the 29th they were ordered to surrender their weapons, an undetermined shot was fired, firing erupted on both sides, in which Big Foot and nearly 200 men, women and children, along with 25 soldiers were killed. Big Foot and his followers killed during the battle are buried on a hill overlooking Wounded Knee battlefield.[1]

---

1. www.homeofheros.com
2. www.dickshovel.com/Medals.G.b.html

Appendix # 4 - Fort Laramie Treaty Of 1868

FORT LARAMIE TREATY 1868

ARTICLES OF A TREATY MADE AND CONCLUDED BY AND BETWEEN

Lieutenant General William T. Sherman, General William S. Harney, General Alfred H. Terry, General O. O. Augur, J. B. Henderson, Nathaniel G. Taylor, John G. Sanborn, and Samuel F. Tappan, duly appointed commissioners on the part of the United States, and the different bands of the Sioux Nation of Indians, by their chiefs and headmen, whose names are hereto subscribed, they being duly authorized to act in the premises.

ARTICLE I.

From this day, forward all war between the parties to this agreement shall forever cease. The government of the United States desires peace, and its honor is hereby pledged to keep it. The Indians desire peace and they now pledge their honor to maintain it.

If bad men among the whites, or among other people subject to the authority of the United States, shall commit any wrong upon the person or property of the Indians, the United

States will, upon proof made to the agent, and forwarded to the Commisioner of Indian Affairs at Washington city, proceed at once to cause the offender to be arrested and punished according to the laws of the United States, and also reimburse the injured person for the loss sustained.

If bad men among the Indians shall commit a wrong or depredation upon the person or property of nay one, white, black, or Indian, subject to the authority of the United States, and at peace therewith, the Indians herein named solemnly agree that they will, upon proof made to their agent, and notice by him, deliver up the wrongdoer to the United States, to be tried and punished according to its laws, and, in case they willfully refuse so to do, the person injured shall be reimbursed for his loss from the annuities, or other moneys due or to become due to them under this or other treaties made with the United States; and the President, on advising with the Commissioner of Indian Affairs, shall prescribe such rules and regulations for ascertaining damages under the provisions of this article as in his judgment may be proper, but no one sustaining loss while violating the provisions of this treaty, or the laws of the United States, shall be reimbursed therefore.

ARTICLE II.

The United States agrees that the following district of country, to wit, viz: commencing on the east bank of the Missouri river where the 46th parallel of north latitude crosses the same, thence along low-water mark down said east bank to a point opposite where the northern line of the State of Nebraska strikes the river, thence west across said river, and along the northern line of Nebraska to the 104th degree of longitude west from Greenwich, thence north on said meridian to a point where the 46th parallel of north latitude intercepts the same, thence due east along said parallel to the place of beginning; and in addition thereto, all existing reservations of the east back of said river, shall be and the same is, set apart for the absolute and undisturbed use and occupation of the

Indians herein named, and for such other friendly tribes or individual Indians as from time to time they may be willing, with the consent of the United States, to admit amongst them; and the United States now solemnly agrees that no persons, except those herein designated and authorized so to do, and except such officers, agents, and employees of the government as may be authorized to enter upon Indian reservations in discharge of duties enjoined by law, shall ever be permitted to pass over, settle upon, or reside in the territory described in this article, or in such territory as may be added to this reservation for the use of said Indians, and henceforth they will and do hereby relinquish all claims or right in and to any portion of the United States or Territories, except such as is embraced within the limits aforesaid, and except as hereinafter provided.

ARTICLE III.

If it should appear from actual survey or other satisfactory examination of said tract of land that it contains less than 160 acres of tillable land for each person who, at the time, may be authorized to reside on it under the provisions of this treaty, and a very considerable number of such persons shall be disposed to commence cultivating the soil as farmers, the United States agrees to set apart, for the use of said Indians, as herein provided, such additional quantity of arable land, adjoining to said reservation, or as near to the same as it can be obtained, as may be required to provide the necessary amount.

ARTICLE IV.

The United States agrees, at its own proper expense, to construct, at some place on the Missouri river, near the center of said reservation where timber and water may be convenient, the following buildings, to wit, a warehouse, a store-room for the use of the agent in storing goods belonging to the Indians, to cost not less than $2,500; an agency building, for the residence of the agent, to cost not exceeding $3,000; a residence for the physician, to cost not more than $3,000;

and five other buildings, for a carpenter, farmer, blacksmith, miller, and engineer-each to cost not exceeding $2,000; also, a school-house, or mission building, so soon as a sufficient number of children can be induced by the agent to attend school, which shall not cost exceeding $5,000.

The United States agrees further to cause to be erected on said reservation, near the other buildings herein authorized, a good steam circular saw-mill, with a grist-mill and shingle machine attached to the same, to cost not exceeding $8,000.

ARTICLE V.

The United States agrees that the agent for said Indians shall in the future make his home at the agency building; that he shall reside among them, and keep an office open at all times for the purpose of prompt and diligent inquiry into such matters of complaint by and against the Indians as may be presented for investigation under the provisions of their treaty stipulations, as also for the faithful discharge of other duties enjoined on him by law. In all cases of depredation on person or property he shall cause the evidence to be taken in writing and forwarded, together with his findings, to the Commissioner of Indian Affairs, whose decision, subject to the revision of the Secretary of the Interior, shall be binding on the parties to this treaty.

ARTICLE VI.

If any individual belonging to said tribes of Indians, or legally incorporated with them, being the head of a family, shall desire to commence farming, he shall have the privilege to select, in the presence and with the assistance of the agent then in charge, a tract of land within said reservation, not exceeding three hundred and twenty acres in extent, which tract, when so selected, certified, and recorded in the "Land Book" as herein directed, shall cease to be held in common, but the same may be occupied and held in the exclusive possession of the person selecting it, and of his family, so long as he or they may continue to cultivate it.

Any person over eighteen years of age, not being the head of a family, may in like manner select and cause to be certified to him or her, for purposes of cultivation, a quantity of land, not exceeding eighty acres in extent, and thereupon be entitled to the exclusive possession of the same as above directed.

For each tract of land so selected a certificate, containing a description thereof and the name of the person selecting it, with a certificate endorsed thereon that the same has been recorded, shall be delivered to the party entitled to it, by the agent, after the same shall have been recorded by him in a book to be kept in his office, subject to inspection, which said book shall be known as the "Sioux Land Book."

The President may, at any time, order a survey of the reservation, and, when so surveyed, Congress shall provide for protecting the rights of said settlers in their improvements, and may fix the character of the title held by each. The United States may pass such laws on the subject of alienation and descent of property between the Indians and their descendants as may be thought proper. And it is further stipulated that any male Indians over eighteen years of age, of any band or tribe that is or shall hereafter become a party to this treaty, who now is or who shall hereafter become a resident or occupant of any reservation or territory not included in the tract of country designated and described in this treaty for the permanent home of the Indians, which is not mineral land, nor reserved by the United States for special purposes other than Indian occupation, and who shall have made improvements thereon of the value of two hundred dollars or more, and continuously occupied the same as a homestead for the term of three years, shall be entitled to receive from the United States a patent for one hundred and sixty acres of land including his said improvements, the same to be in the form of the legal subdivisions of the surveys of the public lands. Upon application in writing, sustained by the proof of two disinterested witnesses, made to the register of the local land office when the land sought to be entered is within a land district, and when the tract sought to be entered is not in any land district, then upon said application and proof being made to the Commissioner of the General Land Office, and the right of such Indian or Indians to enter such tract or tracts of land shall accrue and be perfect from the date of his first improvements thereon, and shall continue as long as be continues his residence and improvements and no longer. And any Indian or Indians receiving a patent for land under the foregoing provisions shall thereby and from thenceforth become and be a citizen of the United States and be entitled to all the privileges and immunities of such citizens, and shall, at the same time, retain all his rights to benefits accruing to Indians under this treaty.

ARTICLE VII.

In order to insure the civilization of the Indians entering into this treaty, the necessity of education is admitted, especially of such of them as are or may be settled on said agricultural reservations, and they, therefore, pledge themselves to compel their children, male and female, between the ages of six and sixteen years, to attend school, and it is hereby made the duty of the agent for said Indians to see that this stipulation is strictly complied with; and the United States agrees that for every thirty children between said ages, who can be induced or compelled to attend school, a house shall be provided, and a teacher competent to teach the elementary branches of an English education shall be furnished, who will reside among said Indians and faithfully discharge his or her duties as a teacher. The provisions of this article to continue for not less than twenty years.

ARTICLE VIII.

When the head of a family or lodge shall have selected lands and received his certificate as above directed, and the agent shall be satisfied that he intends in good faith to commence cultivating the soil for a living, he shall be entitled to receive seeds and agricultural implements for the first year, not exceeding in value one hundred dollars, and for each succeeding year he shall continue to farm, for a period of three years more, he shall be entitled to receive seeds and implements as aforesaid, not exceeding in value twenty-five dollars. And it is further stipulated that such persons as commence farming shall receive instruction from the farmer herein provided for, and whenever more than one hundred persons shall enter upon the cultivation of the soil, a second blacksmith shall be provided, with such iron, steel, and other material as may be needed.

ARTICLE IX.

At any time after ten years from the making of this treaty, the United States shall have the privilege of withdrawing the physician, farmer, blacksmith, carpenter, engineer, and miller herein provided for, but in case of such withdrawal, an additional sum thereafter of ten thousand dollars per annum shall be devoted to the education of said Indians, and the Commissioner of Indian Affairs shall, upon careful inquiry into their condition, make such rules and regulations for the expenditure of said sums as will best promote the education and moral improvement of said tribes.

ARTICLE X.

In lieu of all sums of money or other annuities provided to be paid to the Indians herein named under any treaty or treaties heretofore made, the United States agrees to deliver at the agency house on the reservation herein named, on or before the first day of August of each year, for thirty years, the following articles, to wit:

For each male person over 14 years of age, a suit of good substantial woolen clothing, consisting of coat, pantaloons, flannel shirt, hat, and a pair of home-made socks.

For each female over 12 years of age, a flannel shirt, or the goods necessary to make it, a pair of woolen hose, 12 yards of calico, and 12 yards of cotton domestics.

For the boys and girls under the ages named, such flannel and cotton goods as may be needed to make each a suit as aforesaid, together with a pair of woolen hose for each.

And in order that the Commissioner of Indian Affairs may be able to estimate properly for the articles herein named, it shall be the duty of the agent each year to forward to him a full and exact census of the Indians, on which the estimate from year to year can be based.

And in addition to the clothing herein named, the sum of $10 for each person entitled to the beneficial effects of this treaty shall be annually appropriated for a period of 30 years, while such persons roam and hunt, and $20 for each person who engages in farming, to be used by the Secretary of the Interior in the purchase of such articles as from time to time the condition and necessities of the Indians may indicate to be proper. And if within the 30 years, at any time, it shall appear that the amount of money needed for clothing, under this article, can be appropriated to better uses for the Indians named herein, Congress may, by law, change the appropriation to other purposes, but in no event shall the amount of the appropriation be withdrawn or discontinued for the period named. And the President shall annually detail an officer of the army to be present and attest the delivery of all the goods herein named, to the Indians, and he shall inspect and report on the quantity and quality of the goods and the manner of their delivery. And it is hereby expressly stipulated that each Indian over the age of four years, who shall have removed to and settled permanently upon said reservation, one pound of meat and one pound of flour per day, provided the Indians cannot furnish their own subsistence at an earlier date. And it is further stipulated that the United States will furnish and deliver to each lodge of Indians or family of persons legally incorporated with the, who shall remove to the reservation herein described and commence farming, one good American cow, and one good well-broken pair of American oxen within 60 days after such lodge or family shall have so settled upon said reservation.

ARTICLE XI.

In consideration of the advantages and benefits conferred by this treaty and the many pledges of friendship by the United States, the tribes who are parties to this agreement hereby stipulate that they will relinquish all right to occupy permanently the territory outside their reservations as herein defined, but yet reserve the right to hunt on any lands north of North Platte, and on the Republican Fork of the Smoky Hill river, so long as the buffalo may range thereon in such numbers as to justify the chase. And they, the said Indians, further expressly agree:

1st. That they will withdraw all opposition to the construction of the railroads now being built on the plains.

2d. That they will permit the peaceful construction of any railroad not passing over their reservation as herein defined.

3d. That they will not attack any persons at home, or traveling, nor molest or disturb any wagon trains, coaches, mules, or cattle belonging to the people of the United States, or to persons friendly therewith.

4th. They will never capture, or carry off from the settlements, white women or children.

5th. They will never kill or scalp white men, nor attempt to do them harm.

6th. They withdraw all pretence of opposition to the construction of the railroad now being built along the Platte river and westward to the Pacific ocean, and they will not in future object to the construction of railroads, wagon roads, mail stations, or other works of utility or necessity, which may be ordered or permitted by the laws of the United States. But should such roads or other works be constructed on the lands of their reservation, the government will pay the tribe whatever amount of damage may be assessed by three disinterested commissioners to be appointed by the President for that purpose, one of the said commissioners to be a chief or headman of the tribe.

7th. They agree to withdraw all opposition to the military posts or roads now established south of the North Platte river, or that may be established, not in violation of treaties heretofore made or hereafter to be made with any of the Indian tribes.

ARTICLE XII.

No treaty for the cession of any portion or part of the reservation herein described which may be held in common, shall be of any validity or force as against the said Indians unless executed and signed by at least three-fourths of all the adult male Indians occupying or interested in the same, and no cession by the tribe shall be understood or construed in such manner as to deprive, without his consent, any individual member of the tribe of his rights to any tract of land selected by him as provided in Article VI of this treaty.

ARTICLE XIII.

The United States hereby agrees to furnish annually to the Indians the physician, teachers, carpenter, miller, engineer, farmer, and blacksmiths, as herein contemplated, and that such appropriations shall be made from time to time, on the estimate of the Secretary of the Interior, as will be sufficient to employ such persons.

ARTICLE XIV.

It is agreed that the sum of five hundred dollars annually for three years from date shall be expended in presents to the ten persons of said tribe who in the judgment of the agent may grow the most valuable crops for the respective year.

ARTICLE XV.

The Indians herein named agree that when the agency house and other buildings shall be constructed on the reservation named, they will regard said reservation their permanent home, and they will make no permanent settlement elsewhere; but they shall have the right, subject to the conditions and modifications of this treaty, to hunt, as stipulated in Article XI hereof.

ARTICLE XVI.

The United States hereby agrees and stipulates that the country north of the North Platte river and east of the summits of the Big Horn mountains shall be held and considered to be unceded. Indian territory, and also stipulates and agrees that no white person or persons shall be permitted to settle upon or occupy any portion of the same; or without the consent of the Indians, first had and obtained, to pass through the same; and it is further agreed by the United States, that within ninety days after the conclusion of peace with all the bands of the Sioux nation, the military posts now established in the territory in this article named shall be abandoned, and that the road leading to them and by them to the settlements in the Territory of Montana shall be closed.

ARTICLE XVII.

It is hereby expressly understood and agreed by and between the respective parties to this treaty that the execution of this treaty and its ratification by the United States Senate shall have the effect, and shall be construed as abrogating and annulling all treaties and agreements heretofore entered into between the respective parties hereto, so far as such treaties and agreements obligate the United States to furnish and provide money, clothing, or other articles of property to such Indians and bands of Indians as become parties to this treaty, but no further.

In testimony of all which, we, the said commissioners, and we, the chiefs and headmen of the Brule band of the Sioux nation, have hereunto set our hands and seals at Fort Laramie, Dakota Territory, this twenty-ninth day of April, in the year one thousand eight hundred and sixty-eight.

Signed by 8 Government Officials including 4 General Officers

Signed by 25 Brule Sioux Band Chief's on April 29, 1868

Signed by 38 Oglala Sioux Band Chief's on May 25, 1868

Signed by 16 Minneconjou Sioux Band Chief's on May 25, 1868

Signed by 22 Yanctonais Sioux Band Chief' on May 25, 1868

Signed by 26 Arapahoes Chief's on May 25, 1868

Signed by 6 Sioux Reservation Chief's on November 6, 1868 [1]

---

1. http://puffin.crighton.edu/lakota/1868_la.html

Appendix # 5 Bibliography

1. www.his.state.mt.us/departments/Library-Archives/Pamphlets/custer.html
2. www.fs.fed.us/npnht/old/bibliography/govdoc.htm- Government Documents
3. www.scsc.k12.ar.us/2003outwest/HendersonC/
4. www.philkearny.vcn.com/fpk-overview.htm
5. www.wyomingbnb-ranchrec.com/History.FettermanFight.html
6. www.wyomingbnb-ranchrec.com/History.WagonBox.html
7. www.scsc.k12.ar.us/2003outwest/LachowskyR/FortLaramie.htm
8. www.wyoshpo.state.wy.us/crazy.htm
9. www.americanindian.net/2003n.html
10. www.nps.gov/fola/Fort_Davis_WEB_PAGE/About_theFort/Fetterman_battlefield.hmt
11. www.geocities.com/braintanning/oglala.html
12. www.wyoshpo.state.wy.us/fortreno.htm
13. www.media.utah.edu/UHE/c/CONNOR%2CPATRICK.html
14. www.onlineutah.com/bearrivermassacre.shtml
15. www.wyoshpo.start.wy.us/connor.htm
16. www.nps.gov/foda/Fort_Davis_WEB_PAGE/About_the_fort/Wagon_Box.htm _
17. www.nps.gov/foda/Fort_Davis_WEB_PAGE/About_the_fort/Wounded_Knee.htm ,
18. McDermott, Circle of Fire, Indian War of 1865

19. McDermott, General George Crook's 1876 Campaigns
20. McDermott, a Guide to the Indian Wars in the West
21. O'Neal, Fighting Men of the Indian War
22. Keenan, The Wagon Box Fight
23. Murray, The Bozeman Trail
24. Warner, Ferd H., The Dull Knife Battle
25. Haines, Historical Along the Oregon Trail
26. Hedren, Paul L., First Scalp to Custer
27. Green, Jerome A., Slim Buttes 1876
28. Morgan, R. Kent, Our Hallowed Ground, Guide to Indian War Battlefield Locations in Eastern Montana

About the Author

The author was born and raised in Beardstown, Illinois. Service in Naval Aviation and Viet Nam Veteran, 1965.

Lives in Seattle, married, three children, BA from Univ. of Wash., 1974, with Duel MBA's from City University, 2000.

Became interested in history at a young age, when collecting WWI and II items with my father, Jacob P. Morgan.

Began reading the Plainsmen Series by the late Terry C. Johnston, which captivated my interest in the Indian Wars. Read extensively, research, locate, and walk the Indian War Battlefields in Montana, Wyoming, North & South Dakota and Nebraska. The richness for me is the research and then walking these Hallowed Grounds.

Any journey always begins with…the first step!